# Spiritual Intelligence at Work

## A RADICAL Approach to Increasing Productivity, Raising Morale and Preventing Conflict

**COLIN C. TIPPING**

Award-winning Author of *RADICAL Forgiveness: Making Room for the Miracle*

## Spiritual Intelligence at Work

A RADICAL Approach to Increasing Productivity, Raising Morale, and Preventing Conflict

Published in July, 2004

*The Quantum Energy Management System*
is a trademark owned by Colin Tipping.

**ISBN** 0-9704814-4-6

Global 13 Publications, Inc.
26 Briar Gate Lane,
Marietta GA 30066
sales@radicalforgiveness.com

**Website: www.radicalforgiveness.com**
Cover Design: Deborah Hill
Illustrations: JoAnna Tipping
Copyeditor: Beth Phillips

# Contents

iii

# ILLUSTRATIONS

# Preface

One of the great lessons I learned when I wrote and published my first book in 1997 was the importance of having just the right title.

With that in mind, I must confess that I had a great deal of trepidation about giving a corporate book a title that included the word "spiritual." Almost all the corporate consultants I talked to about writing this book advised me to stay away from using such words, even in the main body of the book, let alone in the title!

And yet, I am sure you will agree that, while the word "spiritual" implies being *not of this world*, the term "spiritual intelligence" has an altogether more worldly and practical ring to it, following logically as it does from the other two accepted forms of intelligence, intellectual and emotional.

Both intellectual and emotional intelligence are now part of the normal vocabulary of both the science and the practice of modern management, so it is surely not pushing the envelope too far to suggest that there might be some benefit in looking more closely at this other down-to-earth attribute that all human beings possess — spiritual intelligence — and seeing how it might be used to good advantage.

In 1997, I wrote and published the book, *RADICAL Forgiveness: Making Room for the Miracle,* that proposed a form of forgiveness which was totally different from the traditional version of forgiveness that most people understood then to be the only kind. Radical Forgiveness turned out to be — in stark contrast to traditional forgiveness — easy to do, simple to effect and almost instantaneous in its result. I have been doing workshops around the world using this particular technology since then, and it has changed the lives of many thousands of people.

Radical Forgiveness was so successful because it did not rely on, or even reference, the traditional psychological therapeutic approach to forgiveness. Neither did it identify with the other-worldly spiritual approach to forgiveness with its meditations, guided visualizations and other "special" techniques that don't work. No, it was amazingly successful in spite of its apparent simplicity because it called upon and utilized the person's innate spiritual intelligence.

I say innate because I believe that it is something we all have — and in roughly equal proportion. It's just that we have tended to ignore spiritual intelligence and have downplayed its importance in favor of intellectual intelligence. Not that it is in competition with intellectual or even emotional intelligence. All three are complementary.

Having proved that Radical Forgiveness works, I am now using a similar version of the technology as a form of conflict resolution and prevention within organizations. This version not only has the same ease and simplicity to it but the same dramatically high level of success. It is called the Quantum Energy Management System (QEMS). The book you now have in your hands sets out the rationale for this system.

Just as Radical Forgiveness was able to lift traditional forgiveness to a whole new level using spiritual intelligence — making something that was universally considered to be extremely difficult to achieve, easy, quick and simple — the QEMS is taking conflict resolution and discord prevention to a whole new level in exactly the same way.

A concept closely tied to the idea of spiritual intelligence is that of energy, life-force energy. Spiritual intelligence appears to use this energy in ways that, as yet, we do not fully understand. *(Having said that, it does seem that quantum physicists have a pretty good handle on it — hence our name, Quantum Energy Management System).*

All living things possess this energy. Likewise, so do organizations. The energy of a corporation, institution or bureaucracy is the sum total of the energy contributed by every individual in the organization. *(An example of a corporation with high energy would be Southwest Airlines).* The objective of the QEMS is to enable each individual in the company to keep their own energy in positive balance, thereby contributing to the overall balance of the energy field of the organization.

The form of energy I am particularly interested in, that has the potential to create havoc within any organization, and for which, up to now there has been no antidote, is what I am calling *humanergy.* This is a term I have coined to describe subtle human energy that everyone in the company has to a greater or lesser degree and that emanates from deep in the subconscious mind. It is energy that has up to now been impossible to identify — let alone control or manage.

Fortunately, we now have the means to do both, and excitingly, it has turned out that spiritual intelligence is the key. The potential for a corporation to save a great deal of money by learning how to manage humanergy is enormous.

I have structured this book in recognition of the fact that some people prefer to gain knowledge and understanding in a logical, linear, left-brain-oriented way while others like to learn through stories. In order to cater to each learning style, I am presenting the material in both didactic and story form.

But rather than indicate a bias by beginning with one or the other, I have made them run conconcurrently, with the story running on the left page and the logic running on the right page. This might feel a little awkward at first, but you'll soon adjust. It doesn't matter which you read first, but I can assure you that the whole idea will come much more into focus if you read both before moving on to Part Two.

The story, which can be also obtained in audio form on a CD or downloaded from our web site, is a tale about a fictitious company that shows exactly what happens when the latent forms of humanergy of some of the employees conspire to create problems that affect the company as a whole and then what happens when they are introduced to the concepts contained in this book. I think you will find it extremely interesting and revealing. You may even recognize yourself in it!

Enjoy!

Colin Tipping                                              June 2004

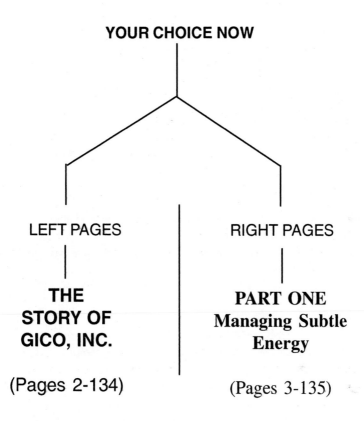

**YOUR CHOICE NOW**

**LEFT PAGES**

**THE STORY OF GICO, INC.**

(Pages 2-134)

**RIGHT PAGES**

**PART ONE Managing Subtle Energy**

(Pages 3-135)

**Note:** Don't try reading them simultaneously. Read the story or Part One through first, then go back and read the other.

Read with an open mind and a willingness to have your existing ideas and beliefs challenged.

ENJOY!

# The Gico Story

I t was Bob's fiftieth birthday. Nevertheless, he was making his way to the office at his normal hour. He liked to be at his desk by 6:45 A.M., every day, which meant departing from home at around 6:15, leaving Jean and the two kids still fast asleep. That way, he could avoid the morning traffic and get a decent amount of work done before the general hubbub of the working day began with all its demands, pressures and distractions. Also, being something of a loner, he liked to have at least some part of the day to himself.

As usual, Mrs. Harper, his secretary, arrived on time at 8:30 A.M. She was the only one who knew that it was his birthday. Bob had told her explicitly that he did not want a party or anything like that, nor even that anyone else should know that it was his birthday — especially his fiftieth. He didn't feel like celebrating anything, so he'd much rather it went unnoticed.

Bob was a little below average height with a slim athletic build. His hair was mostly thick and dark except for graying temples. You might not, at first glance, take him for fifty. Where he really did show his age, though, was around the eyes. Deeply set and ice blue, they were not at all easy to see beneath his bushy eyebrows, which were knitted into a perpetual frown — obviously the result of many years of stress and worry. His finely chiselled face and open smile made up for it though. He was really quite handsome.

Still, he was not feeling good about reaching fifty and didn't want attention brought to the fact. He just wanted the day to pass unnoticed, and to be like any other ordinary day. In fact, Bob was feeling more depressed than normal and didn't really know why. For the last six months he had been feeling very disturbed, as if something were gnawing at him from the inside.

**Caution:** *Don't try to read the Gico story at the same time as you read this part. Some people attempted to do just that and it fried their brains! Read one or the other, in their entirety, first.*

# 1
# Humanergy

Imagine, if you will, a corporation as being analogous to a living organism. Then equate the teams of people within an organization to the complex molecules making up the organism, and see each individual person in the organization as the equivalent of a single atom — the basic building block.

In the typical corporation we might easily find the counterparts of the systems of a living organism. For the skeletal, vascular, digestive and nervous systems of a living organism, substitute the elements of a typical corporate structure — infrastructure, buildings, machinery, communication systems and so on. Then equate the blood, nutrients, hormones and other fluids that move through the body, delivering energy to every part of it, to those elements that flow through the "arteries and veins" of a corporation, giving it energy and life — materials, data, ideas, money, etc.

Living organisms are energetic in nature. They have an invisible lifeforce and an energy field peculiar to each one. In fact, biologists now think of organisms, not so much as a bunch of chemicals and molecules, but as a complex matrix of interrelating energy fields. It is equally helpful, I believe, to look at corporations in this way and to analyze them in terms of how well the energy actually flows within the structure.

He had had similar experiences in the past but had always managed to push the feelings away by immersing himself in his work. As president of the company he always had a mountain of work that he never could get the better of, so it had always been easy for him to bury those feelings by working long hours.

This time it didn't seem to be working. Lately he was finding himself unable to really focus on his work, becoming indecisive and reclusive. He was biting people's heads off and being demanding and critical of, and really hard on, the very people on whom he depended.

Throughout the company, people were talking about it, and many of them were beginning to wonder whether their boss was really up to the job. It wasn't just affecting the senior management team who had to deal with him every day. It was trickling down the ranks and affecting morale throughout the entire firm.

It is still possible in a company employing fifty people to have something akin to a family atmosphere, especially when, as was the case with Gico Inc., many of the employees had been there for several years, having been promoted up through the ranks. In Gico's case, this had produced a loyalty and a synergy that had worked really well over the years. But as with any extended family, if one part becomes dysfunctional, everyone senses it, and it becomes a major disturbance throughout.

One such disturbance had occurred five years earlier when the man who had been president of the company for the last thirty-five years retired, and contrary to expectations, the board appointed someone from outside the company. That person was, of course, Bob Pearson. There were at least two people at Gico who had coveted that job for many years, both of whom probably would have accepted the appointment of the other with equanimity. So when an outsider was appointed, the two contenders were both flabbergasted and enraged. They felt totally betrayed. One of them took early retirement and left. He died within the year.

## Corporate Energy Flow

There are four main forms of energy flowing through any corporation. These are:

1. Data
2. Materials
3. Money
4. Human Energy (Humanergy) — *Subtle Energy*

If the flow of any one of these is impeded, the result is bound to be decreased efficiency and output with a corresponding negative effect on the bottom line.

## Gross Energy

As indicated above, data, money and materials are **gross** energies. They are subject to clear definition, accurate measurement, record keeping and control. Each one of these has its own channel through which it moves and its own system by which the flow can be accurately monitored. Through the use of sophisticated systems based on computer technology, it is probably fair to say that business has more or less mastered the flow of gross energy.

## Subtle Energy

*Humanergy,* * on the other hand, is *subtle* energy and it is not susceptible at all to measurement or control. It operates below the level of conscious awareness and, with the exception of some that manifests outwardly at the physical end of the scale, its effects cannot be directly observed. It not only emanates from each individual human being in the corporation, but from whole groups of human beings, such as work groups, unions, departments within the corporation, the board room, shareholders and so on.

---

*I have coined the word *humanergy* to describe this kind of subtle energy since there does not seem to be a word in existence that describes it in such a way as to facilitate useful discussion in the context of human resources management.

5

Bob's appointment also split the company, since those loyal to the contenders were openly hostile to Bob and were uncooperative for at least the first two years. In many parts of the company the wound still festered, even after five years.

Dennis Barker, the other contender for the job that Bob landed, did not leave the company. As vice president of sales and marketing, he was, in effect, Bob's number two, but it was clear that he considered himself superior to Bob, both in intellect and experience. He made an effort to be a good number two, but it actually wasn't in him to be satisfied with that position. He always wanted to be number one. Bob could sense the resentment that was just beneath the surface, and Dennis would covertly act it out. He would find ways to withhold important information from Bob or to subtly undermine him in the minds of the management team.

The sabotage was never overt enough for Bob to be able to challenge him, for Dennis was too clever to leave himself open to that, but the passive-aggressive behavior was always there. He also never lost an opportunity to finesse Bob in a way that confirmed for him — and for Bob too, truth be known — his superiority.

Dennis was physically overpowering as well. He weighed at least a hundred pounds more than Bob, and at six feet three inches, he towered over Bob, who was only five feet eight inches tall. But whereas Bob moved quickly and easily, Dennis was lumbering and slow by comparison; he also had a very slight stoop.

Even though Bob never let it show, he despised Dennis. He couldn't stand Dennis' false servility and insatiable need for approval. He felt Dennis was inauthentic and untrustworthy and saw him as the stereotypical sales type — great on the surface but with little substance beneath. He saw Dennis as manipulative, self-centered and needy.

Bob did pretty well in disguising these feelings, and to an outside eye, their relationship might seem cordial and even mutually respectful.

## Fields of Humanergy

Humanergy tends to organize itself in complex interrelating fields. Biologist Rupert Sheldrake refers to these fields as morphogenetic fields. These are fields of energy that range from being specific to an individual person to including everyone. If we continue with our analogy of a corporation being a complex living organism, it too would have its own morphogenetic field.

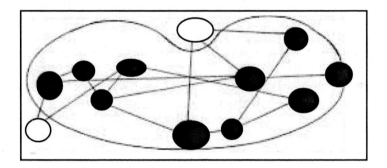

**Fig. 1**: A Morphogenetic Field

Each level and each department within the corporation would also have its own field as would each individual within the corporation. Groups of people (teams, departments, subcontractors, sections, unions, management, executives, shareholders) would also have their own collective energy fields. All of these fields would be in dynamic interaction with each other all the time, creating an ever-changing pattern and an interactive flow of energy.

To understand this idea more clearly, try visualizing the basic energy field of the corporation as being a very still lake. Then imagine someone dropping a stone into the middle of the lake and watch the ripples spreading out until they reach the farthest bank. Let this be the equivalent of the CEO's personal energy field being superimposed on the larger energy field of the corporation.

But those who worked closely with the two of them knew better. They could feel the energy between them, and it was not good. Though it drained energy from the team, no one mentioned it — at least not openly and certainly not to Bob or Dennis.

# Meg

Meg saw her nine year-old daughter Caroline onto the schoolbus at 7:15 A.M. as she normally did, and then got back into the old Honda Civic she had managed to buy from her brother a couple of months before at a really good price. He had upgraded to a new SUV upon getting promoted at work. Knowing that Meg was struggling to make it as a single parent with no child support coming from her ex-husband, he let her have the car on a monthly payment basis. She made the drive to work in about 40 minutes and arrived ready to start work at 8:00 AM.

Meg, having started in the shipping department, had been with Gico for almost 8 years and in that time had progressed up the ladder to become a production supervisor. She was well thought of by those she supervised and, with the exception of one person, by everyone else in the company.

The exception was Monty Fisk, the production manager. For some reason, he had it in for Meg and was making her life miserable. Everything had been fine for the first three years. He would sing her praises and give her all the resources she needed. Then suddenly, after she had been there three years, everything switched. From that point on, nothing was ever right, not only with her but with the people she supervised. He found fault with all of them at every opportunity, so Meg frequently ended up having to defend her staff members against him. They loved her for it, but it put a lot of stress on her and only made her relationship with Monty worse.

Now imagine that it starts to rain. The drops are heavy but widely spaced at first. Each raindrop forms its own pattern of ripples. But these ripples collide with the original set of ripples and then with ripples caused by other raindrops, giving rise to what is known as interference patterns. These patterns can become very complex and apparently chaotic, but they nevertheless have a coherence to them that can be observed.

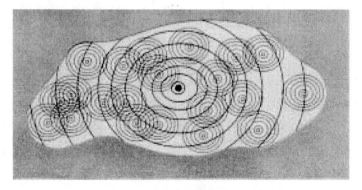

**Fig. 2:** Complex Interrelating Energy Fields

Think of the raindrops as being the various groups and individuals within the corporation. That's what a corporation might look like if we could see the patterns of energy they create as they continually shift and change their own energy fields. Add some wind into the mix (analogous to unexpected and unpredictable events coming from outside the corporation) and imagine how easily those patterns become even more chaotic and disturbed.

Whereas in the past those kinds of complex patterns have been difficult to decipher and to understand and almost impossible to manage, it is the purpose of this book to show that, by using a particular type of technology, called the Quantum Energy Management System (QEMS), they can indeed be tamed and managed quite effectively. Not only that, it can be done in such a way that the need to

He took every opportunity to load her up with additional responsibilities and then set her up to make mistakes so he could find fault with her. Every time an opportunity came up for a possible promotion for Meg, he blocked it. And he would do it in a very perverse way. He knew that she was popular and well thought of, so he couldn't openly bad-mouth her. His strategy was to say that she was so good at what she did and was now carrying so much responsibility that she was indispensable. He would claim that to move her would be extremely detrimental to the department. Somehow, he always managed to convince the executive management that Meg should be neither promoted nor moved sideways out of Monty's reach, a result she had tried on a number of occasions to achieve.

On this particular morning she walked into her department to find people huddled around a certain young woman who was crying. "What's going on?" asked Meg.

"Mr. Fisk really chewed her out in a very nasty way over something that was not her fault and has threatened to put her on performance probation," replied one of Meg's team members. "That man is a pig!"

As Meg garnered as much information as she could about the exchange, she felt the rage building up inside. Why is this man making life so difficult for my staff and me, she thought. It's not fair and I have to put a stop to it now! She stormed into Monty's office. He was waiting for her, leaning way back in his chair, hands clasped behind his head and feet up on the desk, looking triumphant. She slammed the door behind her and stood there fuming, looking at him with eyes ablaze. She was tall, slim, and very attractive, but right then she looked quite capable of killing someone — in this case Monty Fisk.

"Why did you do that to her?" she shouted at him. "You know how she is — how easily upset she can get, and what you accused her of was not legitimate anyway, and you know it. Why do you have to be such a bully?"

actually decipher the precise pattern, or what caused it to form, becomes unnecessary.

## The Humanergy Continuum
Another way to understand the nature of humanergy is to see it as a continuum, with physical human energy at one end of the scale, spiritual energy at the other, and emotional and mental subtle energy in between.

**Fig 3:** The Humanergy Continuum

Depending upon what is sourcing the humanergy, its quality is either coarse or fine. Coarse subtle energy is that which flows from the ego. Fine subtle energy is that which flows from Spirit.

## Spirit
By Spirit we mean that which is indefinable and essentially mysterious but which we feel exists as a supernatural or mystical force in our lives. It is most commonly defined as our *higher power,* and even then it is whatever that may be for each one of us.

We shall be examining this facet of human beingness in Part Three as part of the discussion of that which I call spiritual intelligence. Similar to instinct, spiritual intelligence is something we all have, and more or less to the same degree. It has nothing to do with religion, faith, or any particular belief, nor even with spirituality.

He slowly took his feet off the desk, lowered his large bony hands and stood up. He was a tall, powerfully built man, and he pulled himself up to his full height. His eyes were cold and piercing. "Sit down!" he commanded in a quiet but menacing voice.

She remained standing, breathing heavily, defiant but scared. "Sit down!" he repeated, this time with a good deal more volume. She sank down into the chair. He remained standing with both hands on the desk leaning over towards her and looking down at her.

"Let me tell you something, Meg," he said quietly. "I know you think you are Little Miss Popular around here but I have the measure of you. You came into this company, and you advanced quickly. Do you know why?"

Not waiting for a reply, he went on. "What you don't know is that you only got your promotions because I made them happen. I saw your ability early, and I wanted to have you working for me, so I went out of my way to have you promoted. You have your job for one reason only — because of me. And I can undo what I have done if I have a mind to. I have a lot of clout in this company, Meg, because I get things done and I help them make a lot of money. I've been here a long time, and at this level what I say goes. Understand?"

Meg just sat there, saying nothing yet feeling an intense hatred for this man. He was intimidating her, but she held his gaze. There was a long pause before Monty spoke.

"You did real well for a time, and I was pleased with the way you worked. To a large extent, Meg, I still am, and I wouldn't want to lose you. But you have become too damn cocky, and you constantly try to undermine my authority," continued Monty. "And I won't let you. Do you hear me? I know how you speak to the people out on the shop floor about me, and I notice how you build yourself up to be the Mother Superior around this place. I am in charge around here, Meg, not you! Your are here to do my bidding and to do it the way I tell you to

12

Spiritual intelligence is the finest of subtle energies and, when called upon, is very reliable. When applied to business, it is immensely powerful.

## Ego

Coarse subtle energy emanates from our ego, which is that part of us that imagines we are separate from our Source (God, Higher Intelligence, the Universe, the Creator, the Creative Principle, et cetera). It is that part of ourselves that believes that we are completely individualized, separate and totally in control of everything.

## Humanergy Communication

It is through subtle energy that we attract, repel, bond with and influence other people. It is in fact, a powerful form of communication. To a large degree, industrial psychology has gone a long way towards understanding how subtle energy works, especially with regard to how people relate to each other as individuals and how teams operate within particular contexts.

> **Attracting and Repelling:** If our energies match, we are attracted to each other. If they don't match, we tend to be repelled. We sense a dissonance which is not comfortable, and we move away from each other.

> **Bonding:** This occurs if the match in subtle energy between us is strong, especially if the match is with regard to emotional subtle energy. Our energy fields merge and we feel very connected to each other.

> **Influencing Others with Humanergy:** People whose energy field is strong can influence other people just by their presence. Presidents Lyndon Johnson and Bill Clinton had this ability. You could feel their presence the moment they entered the room. It was as if they filled the room. We

do it. I am tired of your making up your own rules and doing things any way you want. From this point on, you'd better do things the way I say they are to be done, or I might suggest to those in power some changes that you might not like. Do I make myself clear, Meg?"

"Quite clear." said Meg.

"That's good. Now get out there and get back to your job!" said Monty.

# Bob

Bob Pearson was no fool. He was aware that he was slipping, and it made him very fearful. He was seeing a recurring pattern, and he didn't like it.

When an executive search firm had recruited him away from HEH, Inc., he knew it had been timely. While during the first three years of his tenure as president there he had produced substantial growth for the company, the results had been a lot weaker during the last two and were showing a pattern of steady decline. Relationships had deteriorated, and he felt that he might have lost his touch. He appeared to sabotage himself in many instances and was making a lot of poor decisions.

So when the search firm had called and suggested this position at Gico, he had jumped at it. The salary was comparable, so he didn't feel demoted, plus they offered some very rich benefits. Thinking that perhaps a smaller company would suit his management style better, Bob had jumped at the opportunity.

"Happy birthday, Mr. Pearson," said Mrs. Harper in a low voice while slipping an envelope containing a very tasteful birthday card onto his desk. "Per your request, I haven't broadcast the fact of your reaching half a century — though I have to say that you don't look your age —

often refer to this quality as charisma. At the other extreme, you can probably bring to mind people who leave you feeling drained and limp after being in their presence. They suck on your energy and deplete you. We might refer to these as "humanergy vampires."

## Latent Humanergy

Notwithstanding the above manifestations of subtle energy, the kind of subtle energy that this book addresses is that which fuels a very much "below the radar" system of human interaction which is unconscious, nonverbal and unseen. This form of humanergy has a latent quality to it. By that I mean that it is always there but, like a volcano, will only erupt under certain circumstances, and even then in ways that might be hidden and misunderstood.

## Toxic Humanergy

Toxic humanergy is the kind of energy that can poison relationships at work and cause havoc at all levels. *(If you are reading or have read the story that is printed on the left-hand pages of this book, you will understand what I mean).*

Very few people know how to consciously manage toxic humanergy and yet, if properly managed and transformed, it can become a very productive force that will have a huge effect on the bottom line. If left unmanaged, as is normally the case, it can be extremely damaging.

## Subtle Energy Myopia

In the tradition of scientific rationalism, which maintains that if you can't see or measure something it doesn't exist, the corporate world has, until recently, been oblivious to humanergy. This has given rise to a condition which I call *subtle energy myopia* - the inability to perceive (and therefore to manage) the humanergy that constantly moves in and through any organization.

and I don't think anyone else has remembered. You never have been one to make a fuss on your birthday, so nobody thinks much about it. Oh! Look here! Someone else does, though."

She was referring to an e-mail that had come through that morning. Bob usually checked e-mails himself during his early morning routine, but he had been so introspective on this particular day, he hadn't done so. "Somebody from your old firm. Here." She passed him the printout and quickly busied herself so as to avoid any eye contact with her boss.

The e-mail was from Rick Tanner, his old business partner from way back. Bob and Rick had started a marketing business together twenty-five years ago.

As with Bob's later ventures, all had gone well for about three years, and then things started to go south. The business almost went bankrupt, but someone decided to invest in the company and rescue it — but only on the condition that Bob leave. Rick had been the negotiator, and Bob always felt that Rick had engineered his departure.

It had been a huge blow to Bob, and for a long while he struggled to get back on his feet. But he did so eventually and found himself a good position as marketing manager of another firm that, through no fault of his own, subsequently went out of business. He then joined HEH, Inc., an engineering firm, as marketing director and subsequently, became president.

He and Rick were the same age, and although they hadn't been in contact for many years since the breakup, it was apparently the fact of it being their fiftieth that had prompted the e-mail. *"Happy Birthday, Bob. We've both made half a century. Congratulations are in order I think. Call me and let's catch up. Rick."*

This failure is not inconsequential. Humanergy is infused into the overall energy system of any corporation (for good or ill) by every human being who works there, from the CEO down to the lowest paid worker — and its effect is powerful. It has the potential to cripple an organization, and yet by the same token it can, if properly managed, provide great nourishment to the organization, its bottom line, and the individual people within it.

## A Chronic Condition

Subtle energy myopia affects a corporation the way a low grade chronic medical condition affects us as individuals. When we have such a condition we are aware of not feeling well and having all sorts of unexplainable symptoms, but nothing that the doctors do makes any difference. In many cases we just learn to live with it and go through life with a diminished life-force, always feeling below par and often in great discomfort. Millions of people are suffering in this way.

## Symptoms

In a corporation, subtle energy myopia will manifest symptomatically as low morale, poor performance, continual conflict, undercurrents of racial discord, customer dissatisfaction and, in the end, lower-than-expected profits. Just as doctors seem unable to cure the above-mentioned chronic condition, management seems virtually impotent to alter these symptoms using traditional methods.

The myopic aspect is our own inability to perceive a corporation as an *energy* system. We need to shift that perception.

We need to see a corporation, no matter how large or small, as a dynamic living organism, always adapting to its environment while at the same time seeking to modify it. Like every living organism a corporation has a "life force," of its own and its own energy field. That energy field is composed of the energy fields of everyone in the

# Meg

Meg returned to her department seething with rage but feeling powerless. Monty had made it quite clear that he had the power to make things very difficult for her and perhaps even to get her fired. He had the authority to make that happen. Meg knew that. By this time, the worker whom Monty had admonished was back at her station feeling sure that Meg had done all she could on her behalf to put things right with the manager.

But Meg knew different. She had made no headway at all, and she felt as though she had let the woman down. She felt like giving notice right away. "Why should I stay and be treated like dirt," she thought, "just because he feels so insecure and threatened by my efficiency and my ability to get the best out of people?"

This was true about Meg. She certainly had the physical bearing and presence of someone who could command respect, but she also showed a flexibility of approach that enabled the people she supervised to really trust her. This combination of strength and softness did indeed enable her to get productivity out of people in a way that Monty Fisk could never do.

But she quickly realized that leaving Gico was out of the question. That's why she hadn't stood up to Monty. She knew she couldn't leave this company, especially now. Her husband had left her a year ago after four years of marriage, disappearing completely and leaving a lot of debt. He had become very violent and abusive, so she wasn't sorry to see him go, but there was no child support, no weekend visitations to give her a break; nothing. She was completely on her own. Her parents were both dead, and all her brothers and sisters lived in other States. She was trapped, and she knew it.

There was another factor too that was preying on her mind. Even though she was only thirty-five, she knew that her health was not

corporation. The cleaner the energy field of each individual, the more efficient will be the corporation.

**Note:** This technology is applicable to all types of organizations, whether it be a government bureaucracy, hospital, military establishment, nonprofit institution or for-profit corporation, no matter how large or small. In the following chapters, I will, for the sake of ease and continuity, use the term "corporation," but please understand that this is not to exclude any other type of organization.

good. She had had a couple of bouts of chronic fatigue syndrome in the past, and she was sensing that it might be returning. Lately, she was finding herself feeling very low on energy and needing more than a normal amount of sleep.

On the two previous occasions, she had just managed to cope well enough for people not to notice. Fortunately it had not been very severe, but to Meg, who was a single parent working at a stressful job, it had seemed debilitating. During those times she found it necessary to sleep virtually almost every hour that she wasn't working or taking care of the home and Caroline. By doing that, she conserved enough energy to be able to effectively do her job, but by the end of the day she was truly exhausted. Each bout lasted about two months. She had researched the literature on CFS and was very aware that it can become extremely debilitating, so she knew she couldn't afford to lose her health insurance.

Meg had not had an easy life. She came from a pretty dysfunctional family. Her father was an alcoholic, and her mother was obsessive-compulsive and ultra critical. Everything had to be perfect for her, which meant that whatever Meg did was never good enough. However hard she tried to please her mother, she could never win her mother's approval. Meg's mother blamed Meg for everything and, perhaps because Meg was the eldest child, used her as the scapegoat for all the dysfunction within the family.

Meg's father was in and out of work because of his drinking, and he began molesting her when she was three years old. As it is for many girls who are molested by their fathers, she initially found it pleasurable and enjoyed getting the attention from the man she had put on a pedestal and from whom she got no attention at all except in that way.

At the same time, however, the deep knowing that it was wrong and shouldn't be happening would well up inside her and induce terrible

# 2
# It's All Energy Anyway

In Chapter One, we cast a corporation as being analogous to a living body. Taking this another step forward now, whereas science once considered the atom (analagous to the individual worker in the corporation) to be the smallest and most basic element, it became apparent that there were even smaller elements within the atom, like the proton and the electron. Later on, scientists discovered even smaller particles. (We might reasonably equate these particles with the mental, emotional and spiritual aspects of individual workers.)

## String Theory

However, in the most recent search for the very smallest, indivisible unit of matter — the basic building block of life, so to speak — scientists have come to the radical conclusion that these units are not particles at all but infinitely subtle packets of energy called strings. The fundamental nature of matter, therefore, is in fact energy. "It is ALL energy," say the physicists. "There IS nothing else."

String theory is dramatically changing how we look at the physical universe and ourselves within it. Where once we felt totally secure in describing ourselves in terms of atoms, molecules and biochemical systems, we now realize that this is descriptive of ourselves only

guilt and fear. The longer the molestation went on, the worse Meg's feelings became. She was extremely frightened of him, and although she wanted the abuse to stop, she was powerless to do anything about it.

She did what most abuse victims do in this situation: she split herself off and disassociated from what was happening and then repressed the pain. When she was twelve, she tried to tell her mother about the abuse but her mother only became extremely rageful about it and would not listen. She just denied it and then shamed Meg even more for suggesting such a thing. Meg felt totally trapped and abandoned.

Finally, at age sixteen, Meg left home. She basically ran away without telling her parents where she was going, which was no big deal since they were too out-of-it to care anyway. For the next few years she became very promiscuous and totally irresponsible. She tried being in a lesbian relationship for a while, but that didn't work out. At age twenty-four she was badly beaten and raped by a man she met in a bar one night. That incident put her into the hospital for three days, but fortunately, she recognized it as her wake-up call. She decided then to give up drinking and drugs and to really pull her life together. She moved, got a decent job, and began building her life again.

She got married at twenty-five to a man who had seemed decent enough at first, but who very soon became violent and emotionally abusive. He drank heavily, and Meg often feared for her life when he would come home drunk. Her daughter Caroline was from this marriage, but there was doubt about who the father was because Meg had had a short but passionate affair with another man. Her husband never suspected, but Meg became fearful for Caroline's safety as well as her own, so she eventually left that marriage and was divorced at twenty-eight.

She did well on her own for a while but she was lonely and in need of support. The chronic fatigue happened during this time, and it scared her to think that she might not be able to support herself and Caroline.

at a very gross level and that beneath that level of description is one that is infinitely more subtle. We are nothing more than a collection of interrelating energy fields, each of which has its own pattern of coherence and intelligence.

This is exactly what the mystics have been saying for centuries, of course. They have always maintained that everything was energy. Apparently they were able to see beyond physical five-sensory reality, that most of us think of as the only possible one, to the basic underlying pattern of life which mathematicians are just now proving to exist. It is interesting to note that we are now living in an age when ancient mysticism and modern science have come into total alignment with each other. Management science should take note!

## A New Reality
Structures like corporations are always a reflection of the prevailing ideas of the culture that give rise to them. First Einstein and then later the quantum physicists, string theory physicists and holographic theory physicists, have completely redefined the nature of reality and shown Newton's theories to be inadequate.

Having said that, Newton's theories are still useful in that they show us how life works at the level of gross reality and enable us to function quite well in the world. But now, having been given a totally new way to see how reality is constructed, a whole new world has opened up to us.

We are now able to have the best of both worlds. We can use the Newtonian paradigm at the level of physicality and quantum physics at the more subtle, more foundational, levels of reality. We shall come to see how important this idea might be for management and discover the opportunities it opens up for a more open, dynamic and infinitely more productive workplace.

She got married again, mostly for that reason, this time to a man who wasn't exactly abusive but who became emotionally unavailable very soon after the wedding. It was a relationship without passion or interest. It was just dull. Meg wasn't the sort of woman to put up with that so she left him. At thirty-four she found herself alone once more.

Having come out of two failed marriages, Meg pretty much made up her mind that she wasn't going to marry, or even live with, a man again, at least not until Caroline was grown up and gone. "All men are selfish and irresponsible," she would say. "They just use you and dump you, and I just don't want anything to do with any of 'em! I'm fine on my own."

In the year since she had become divorced, she had indeed done pretty well on her own. She had more or less gotten herself out of debt and managed to keep the mortgage paid, run a car, and take care of herself and Caroline. She had progressed in the company and was earning a decent wage. It seemed that the only fly in the ointment was Monty. "Why does he have to make things so difficult for me?" she wondered.

As she sat there in her office thinking about it and still fuming, she wondered aloud how she could get back at him. "Get him fired perhaps. Now wouldn't that be good? Well, no. Can't do that. But I'll make sure he gets no cooperation from me in the future. I'm tired of working hard and making him look good."

The bell indicating that it was time for her department to take a coffee break shook her out of her obsessive thinking about how to get back at Monty. "Gotta get on with the job," she told herself. "But let me get a good strong cup of coffee first!"

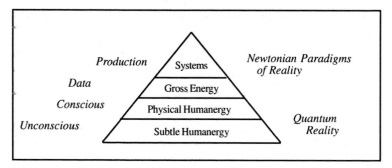

**Fig. 4:** Levels of Reality

On that basis, therefore, we could fairly claim to be in alignment with our present cultural and scientific knowledge if we proclaim that management science needs, on the one hand, to continue paying attention to the gross elements of a corporation while on the other hand, and at the same time, opening its eyes to what is happening at more subtle unseen levels.  In other words, it's time to heal our subtle energy myopia and deepen our understanding of how to manage subtle energy.  Fortunately, we now have the means to do it — and in a way that is easy, simple and very inexpensive.

# Bob

The e-mail had unsettled Bob even more than he already had been before Mrs. Harper had handed it to him. "Why would he write after all these years? Our relationship ended so acrimoniously."

Mrs. Harper was still in earshot but he was really talking to himself. She chose not to respond. Bob felt some pain in the area of his heart and knew it instinctively to be a reminder of the pain of being in that relationship — the pain that he had largely suppressed.

Right from the start Rick had made him feel "less than." No matter how hard he worked or how much effort he put in, it was never enough. Rick found fault with everything he did. Even though they were, in fact, equal partners, Rick had always acted as if he were the boss and had treated Bob accordingly, often making decisions unilaterally.

Where Bob was cautious and conservative, Rick was a risk taker. It was this quality that had gotten the company into deep financial trouble and headed towards bankruptcy. He managed to twist everything around and made it look as if it were all Bob's fault, pointing to Bob's "weak management style" as the cause of the failure. Rick succeeded to the extent that the investors who came in to rescue the company agreed with him and made it a condition of the bailout that Bob had to go. It had been a huge betrayal for Bob. It hadn't helped Bob's self esteem either to learn that, after he left, the company leaped ahead and then years later went public. Rick virtually retired a multimillionaire at age forty-two.

Bob looked again at the e-mail and decided not to take Rick up on the suggestion that they reconnect. The memory of it all was just too much. He crumpled the e-mail very tightly into a ball and tossed it into the trash can. The pain in his chest did not go away.

Mrs. Harper noticed the pained expression on Bob's face but decided to say nothing nor even to let him know that she noticed. She had

# 3
# Medicine & Management Sciences

As evidence of how management science has reflected prevailing societal ideas, it is interesting to review recent history to see how things have changed over the last seventy-five years or so, especially in terms of how the individuals within a corporation have been regarded. Also, as a continuation of our making management science analogous to medical science, we will look at how the two seem to have developed in parallel in this regard.

**Allopathic Medicine and Scientific Management** *(circa 1900 - 1950)* Until quite recently, modern medicine was grounded almost exclusively in the science of biochemistry, making it both mechanistic and reductionist. The body was seen as a complex biochemical machine which was explainable in terms of the behavior of molecules and atoms. When problems arose within the body (disease), the traditional approach was always to intervene at the physical level with such things as surgery or drugs. Because it relied so heavily on the scientific method, which will not acknowledge the veracity of a phenomenon that cannot be measured and verified as real in the physical sense, medical science paid very little attention to the role of mind, emotion and spirit in the causation, healing and prevention of disease.

been working for him for the entire time he had been at the company but had recently found herself having to tiptoe around him all the time, making sure not to get him upset. The president of the company was clearly not himself.

# Monty

Monty was fuming and breathing heavily. It took him quite some time to compose himself after Meg turned her back and walked out of his office, slamming the door hard as she left.

There was something about Meg he just couldn't abide. It seemed that hardly a day passed by where she didn't find some way to get under his skin. Everything she did seemed to upset him — and often to a disproportionate extent . He frequently had to admit that to himself. He also had to concede that she was a good worker who did her job well — there was no doubt about that. The workers adored and respected her because she was both firm and fair. They didn't mess with her, but whenever the need arose, she stood up for them — oftentimes against him. That really angered him.

When she had first joined the company and begun working for him, he had been very comfortable with her. He found her to be teachable and responsive, intelligent and willing to grow into the job. He had liked Meg in the beginning and had vigorously supported her promotion to production supervisor. But as she came into her power and began to exercise more and more responsibility, Monty's feelings began to change. He felt threatened by her. He began to feel that she was undermining him at every opportunity and setting the workers against him. He felt defensive around her, and although she always treated him with due respect, he felt dominated by her in some strange way. She seemed so overpowering!

We might equate this approach with the management techniques that focused on time and motion studies. Here the emphasis was on systems like production lines that have little regard for how workers really feel, or how such things as motivation, team spirit, morale and belief in the company itself — all of which are difficult to measure — might play a role. This style of management, known as scientific management, a term coined in 1911 by Frederick Taylor who was its main proponent, reached its zenith in the 1940's. An era of bitter industrial relations characterized the 50s, as the power of the unions grew and workers demanded better treatment. This shift of power caused management to become more humanistic.

**Holistic Medicine and Human Relations Management** *(circa 1970-1990)*. In recent years we have seen significant changes in both medicine and management. Albeit with some reluctance, medical doctors are now somewhat more willing to acknowledge that people are more than just their bodies and that emotions and mental attitudes do have a role to play in healing. Traditional medicine is very slowly becoming more holistic.

Similarly, management techniques have shifted and now acknowledge the importance of the more subtle human factors mentioned above. Organizing work systems using teams and emphasizing cooperation is one such example of how corporations have become less mechanistic and more humanistic. Many firms are now ready to accept the idea of emotional intelligence and have created ways to build and foster such qualities in their people, especially at management level.

**Energy Medicine and Corporate Energy Flow** *(circa 2000)*
The big change in the medical field, however, has been the rise of a completely nonorthodox kind of medicine based on a very different set of assumptions. Though new to the western mind, this form of medicine has been around for many thousands of years mostly in

Monty sat there at his desk, going over what had just happened, feeling puzzled and perplexed. He never thought of himself as an angry man. So why so much anger? What was it about Meg that upset him so much? He couldn't figure it out at all, other than to assume it was some kind of personality clash. He had to admit that he had chewed that worker out on purpose, knowing that Meg would rise to the bait and come in with guns ablaze, giving him the opportunity to put her down. But he still couldn't quite understand why he needed to do it.

Whatever the reason, Monty resolved to stay on top of her and not let her get the better of him. She had so much support from the workers that she could easily usurp his authority and become, in effect, the boss. He must not allow that to happen. "I need to clip her wings," he said to himself, thinking that it wasn't beyond the bounds of possibility that Meg might threaten his position in the company by causing labor disputes over his leadership style.

"That won't happen," he said as if to comfort himself. "Bob Pearson will support me over her any day." With that he returned to work.

There did in fact exist an unusually close bond between the president and his production manager, such that Monty had every reason to feel more secure in his job than he otherwise might. They had met when they both worked at the company Bob joined after being ejected from his own company by Rick. Bob was a few years older than Monty but saw a great deal of potential in him. Monty was talented and sharp and had a natural flair for organization and production.

While Bob had actually been on the sales and marketing side of that business, he really felt a greater affinity to the manufacturing and production side. In that sense, he was a square peg in a round hole. That being so, he began to derive a vicarious satisfaction from mentoring Monty. Bob used what influence he had at the time to make sure that Monty had ample opportunity to grow in the company during the five years Bob was there.

the Far East. It is called *energy medicine* because it goes beyond the biochemical, scientific, reductionist model of western medicine by focusing on those aspects of us which are not physical in the normal sense of the word but *energetic.*

Energy medicine speaks of a basic animating "life force," that pervades every part of us and without which we would have no life. It recognizes too that this life force is intelligent, is the source of our power and knows how to heal the body and keep it healthy. (**This is spiritual intelligence**).

Energy medicine also sees the body not in terms of atoms and molecules but as a complex web of interrelating energy fields, some of which vibrate slowly enough to manifest as physical matter — atoms and molecules, bones and flesh — but energy fields nonetheless. Energy medicine is holistic in nature since it recognizes that such things as emotion, and what we call spirit, are also energetic in nature and that they interact with all the other fields that constitute who and what we are.

## Correcting Energy Flow to Restore Health

In this model, disease is seen primarily as a blockage of energy, and the business of healing is to unblock it and restore the natural flow throughout the body. This is the basis of modalities such as chiropractic, homeopathy, acupuncture, Healing Touch and many hundreds of other techniques that all seek to restore energetic balance to the organism. Intervention, if carried out at all, does not attempt, as it does in allopathic medicine, to replace or override the body's own system of restoring balance. Rather, it stimulates the body to do what it knows how to do — heal itself through correcting energy flow. It is believed that a body in which energy is flowing properly will not be a fertile environment for germs, parasites, viruses or other pathogens to grow.

31

When Monty eventually applied for and landed another job, Bob felt not only disappointment but a strong sense of betrayal. Monty had not even mentioned that he was looking for another position. Bob knew his feelings were irrational and that he had no right to expect Monty to stay. Nothing was ever said, but Monty felt Bob's disappointment and anger.

He did stay in touch with Bob, if only sporadically and mostly by e-mail. Usually it was just to share some success at work, a promotion perhaps and the contact occurred no more than a couple of times a year.

However, when Monty heard that the president of the company where he worked, Gico, Inc., was retiring and that the likelihood was that either one of two people he despised equally in the company were likely to take his place, he immediately thought of his old mentor, Bob Pearson, who was at that time president of HEH, Inc. Having Bob at the helm of the company where he worked would secure his own position nicely, Monty had reasoned. Monty would do anything to stop Dennis Barker from becoming president. He'd frequently had run-ins with Dennis and knew that if Dennis became president, life might become very precarious.

Dennis Barker was always bitching about how the production department did not keep the sales force properly supported, but as far as Monty was concerned it was Dennis Barker's inefficiency and inability to plan ahead that caused the problems. Dennis treated him with disdain, and Monty could barely bring himself to talk with Dennis.

Monty had dashed off an e-mail letting Bob know that a search firm had been given the task of finding a new president for Gico. He gave Bob a contact number he had somehow acquired and left it at that. Bob took the bait, and the rest was history.

## Allopathic Medicine Denies

The problem for western medicine is that this kind of energy, or life force, is so subtle that it can't be detected by our normal medical instruments and therefore cannot be measured. Their commitment to the scientific method forces doctors to deny the existence of anything until it can be proven to exist, so they ignored it — until, that is, they began to realize that consumers (patients) were taking their custom (and their money) to energy medicine practitioners on an unprecedented scale.

## Educated Consumers Try Energy Medicine

The landmark study that revealed this tendency was reported in the New England Journal of Medicine in January 1993. The author was David Eisenberg, M.D., an internist from Harvard Medical School. He showed that 37% of Americans had used at least one "unconventional" therapy in the previous year. He calculated that in 1991 Americans spent a total of $14 billion on such therapies, with about $5 billion coming directly out of pocket. He also noted that these people were among the most educated of Americans.

Clearly, in 2004, ordinary consumers in their millions are making that same choice in favor of energy medicine and those figures would be much higher now. Since so much money is involved, the medical profession is scrambling to move in that direction as well, but it is still a difficult transition.

## Quantum Healing

Physicists, on the other hand, have no such problem with the idea of there being subtle energies that account for the way our world operates in time and space. That's because physicists long ago gave up Newtonian physics, which is still the basis of medical science, in favor of quantum physics, holographic theory and now, string theory. While such forms of energy medicine such as homeopathy and acupuncture have been around for 7,000 years or more, it is only quite

The debt had only once been acknowledged and, even then, well before Bob took the helm at Gico. From the moment Bob arrived at the firm, Monty had been assiduous in maintaining a careful and respectful distance and had never tried to curry favor with Bob. Neither had Bob resumed his mentoring role, and he treated Monty just like any of his other managers. However, Monty always knew that he had an ace in the hole and that, one day, he might need to make use of it. It gave him a lot of comfort.

# DENNIS

Whenever Dennis Barker entered the room, it was like someone had opened the door and allowed a gust of wind to blow in and completely occupy the space. His energy was enormous, and he got your attention immediately — and yet, there was always something inauthentic about him. One never could feel quite comfortable with him. He was always too eager to please and generous to a fault; people always felt there was another agenda behind everything Dennis said and did. "I've got the figures, Bob," he said as he blew into the room.

"How do they look?" asked Bob with a sinking feeling. He knew they weren't going to be good.

"Not so great," replied Dennis. " We need to talk. Is this a good time? I can come back later if you like."

Bob motioned with his hand for Dennis to sit and held out his hand for the most recent sales figures that Dennis had just prepared. Dennis sat down and drew his chair up closer to Bob's desk. "Oh, and by the way, happy birthday," he said.

Bob peered over his spectacles at Dennis and just grunted, nodding in reluctant acknowledgment. He felt anything but happy. Dennis cast a glance back and gave a shrug as if to say, "Well, I tried."

recently that quantum physics has provided the theoretical under-pinning for them. Hence the term "quantum healing." (You will also now understand why I am using the term "quantum energy management.")

## Corporate Energy Flow

If our medical analogy holds up, we should now be able to see a corporate entity in these terms as well — as a fully functioning living organism that exists as a complex matrix of interrelating energy fields through which energy is constantly flowing. The structure of and all the systems that exist within a corporation should have only one function: to keep that energy flowing through the system as easily and as efficiently as possible. Why? Because, in the end, this subtle energy manifests as money.

## Quantum Energy Management

As "quantum healing" is to medicine, "quantum energy management" is to corporate management in general and human resources management in particular. A quantum energy management system is required to keep the energies within the corporation balanced, finely tuned and flowing as they should. When this is the case, production will be maximized, costs minimized, labor relations refined and energy leaks eliminated. And the people will be happy.

## The Quantum Energy Management System

The Quantum Energy Management System is a technology that we have developed that provides a simple, systems approach to managing humanergy in all its forms. This approach is detailed out in Parts Three and Four of this book and examples of the technology can be found right at the back of the book, along with instructions in how to use one of them in Appendix II. But first, let's learn more about the nature of humanergy and how it works to either enhance or weaken a corporation.

He knew Bob was depressed and struggling to stay together for some reason. Dennis had no idea what was eating Bob but surmised that he and Jean might be having troubles at home. She seemed nice enough, but she liked all the trappings and was always out spending Bob's money at all the finest stores. Perhaps she had gotten him into serious debt. Dennis doubted it though. It seemed Bob was troubled more by what was inside him than by any external circumstances.

Dennis had been watching Bob like a hawk over the last six months and was very aware that Bob was not himself and might even be losing his grip. This might be his chance to replace Bob, he allowed himself to think, but he would need to play his cards very carefully.

"This is just a temporary dip in the figures, Bob," Dennis said, reassuringly. "They'll pick up next quarter for sure. We had so many things not going for us this quarter that will not be factored in next time around. The sales team is much stronger now, and we have built in some good incentives to improve performance."

"With the economy the way it is, we ought to be performing better than this, though," replied Bob as he looked over the figures.

"Bob, you must give yourself credit. Under your leadership, we doubled our net income for each of the first three years of your tenure. That was a tremendous achievement, and I have no doubt in my mind that no one else could have done it *(unspoken subtext: except me, of course)*. I agree it has slowed down somewhat, but it is still good and we are still growing. However, and I hate to say this, Bob, but if we have a problem at all, it is not with sales and marketing but with production."

Bob bristled. Manufacturing and production were his responsibility, and here was Dennis interfering again in his usual manner. He always came on first with the compliments and then hit you from behind with the criticism. Bob immediately snapped back at Dennis, "What are you saying?"

# 4
# Manifest & Latent Humanergy

Some aspects of humanergy show up in a way that is observable and in some cases even measurable. This is *manifest* humanergy. Other aspects of humanergy are neither observable nor measurable and are therefore *latent*.

There are basically four forms of subtle humanergy and each one has its own form of intelligence.

**1.** Manifest and Latent *Physical* Energy     *(Productivity)*
**2.** Manifest and Latent *Mental* Energy     *(Mental I.Q.)*
**3.** Manifest and Latent *Emotional* Energy     *(Emotional I.Q.)*
**4.** Manifest and Latent *Spiritual* Energy     *(Spiritual I.Q.)*

Management science has mastered the intricacies of the manifest forms of the first three but not of the latent forms. It has all but ignored the fourth in both its manifest and latent forms.

Management science has not dabbled very much in the latent forms of any of the four, since to do so would be working with subconscious and unconscious processes — not usually the province of human resource managers.

Dennis knew he was on dangerous ground and would have to tread carefully, but he had seen an opportunity. "We need to modernize our systems, Bob. Our costs are much higher than our competitors', and yet we still have to compete on price and service. The sales people are very frustrated because we are consistently unable to supply the product in a timely fashion and they lose sales as a result of that."

"I'm ahead of you on this, Dennis," replied Bob. "I have already asked Monty Fisk to submit ideas for modernizing the plant."

Dennis leaned forward in his seat, not looking at Bob but at his own feet with his hands tightly clasped together between his legs. He knew how to use his energy to create presence. Pausing for quite some time, he finally looked at Bob and said, "But Monty Fisk is the problem, Bob."

"What the hell do you mean?" Bob responded angrily. "Monty Fisk is a hell of a good production manager."

In his spare time Dennis was a fly fisherman and a good one at that. Now he felt almost as if he were playing Bob like a fish on a line. Bob had taken the bait and now Dennis had to carefully reel him in.

Though Bob didn't realize it, Dennis knew only too well that Monty Fisk had tipped him off about the opening for president and was, in that sense, at least partly responsible for Dennis not getting the job. He hated Fisk, so there was a score to settle there too — but of course Bob, or rather his job, was the bigger fish. He was using a 'minnow to catch a mackerel,' as they say, and it would be sweet revenge indeed if he could dispose of them both at the same time.

Not only did he know of their connection and the debt that Bob owed Monty, but having done his homework well, he had discovered the relationship that Monty and Bob shared as a result of Bob's having mentored Monty for some years. That added another whole dimension to the situation and further ammunition.

However, to ignore the latent forms of humanergy is to ignore the enormous potential that each of them has to either enhance or block the overall flow of energy within the corporation to either the detriment of, or the benefit to, the bottom line. But how can this problem be solved without the need for human resource specialists to have traditional therapeutic skills that would enable them to deal with unconscious repressed material?

### Spiritual Intelligence the Key

That problem has been solved. The Quantum Energy Management System uses a technology that doesn't require the HR person to deal with repressed material. Even the person trained in the QEMS doesn't need therapeutic skills. We have found that the best form of intelligence to use in dealing with the intricacies of both the subconscious mind and the unconscious mind — most especially in the area of conflict resolution — is one's own innate spiritual intelligence.

That might seem surprising. You would think that applied mental intelligence in the form of industrial or organizational psychology would be the obvious discipline to use. Not so. Though it has given us wonderful tools to use in the area of manifest mental energy, such as motivation, communications and cognition, it has not provided us with simple tools that address emotional and mental issues emanating from deep within the subconscious and the unconscious mind.

### The Need for QEMS

As I said at the close of Chapter Three, I will explain the Quantum Energy Management System more fully in Parts Three and Four and in Appendix II. First I will demonstrate the need for it by outlining the nature of each of the forms of humanergy and how they interact dynamically, for good or ill, in the workplace.

"He's of the old school, Bob," replied Dennis softly. "He won't modernize — he's too stuck in his ways. He doesn't understand computers and is unable to hold a vision big enough to spearhead the kind of improvements needed to support the kind of growth we need to have if we want to keep our market share. Our competitors are way ahead of us in terms of efficiency and profitability, Bob, and you know it. We've been putting off the modernizing plan for some time now, to the point where some drastic action is required."

"You might be surprised!" Bob countered. "He'll be reporting to me with his suggestions for modernization by the end of this month. As soon as we have them, we'll have a meeting to discuss them. Until then, the subject is closed! Now, if there's nothing else, Dennis, I need to get back to work."

Clearly, the meeting was at an end, but Dennis felt pleased with the limited outcome of this exchange and, with all due deference, gracefully made his exit.

Dennis was a patient man but he was also driven. He wanted Bob's job so much he could taste it. He had watched Bob build the company fast in his first three years but was now recognizing the signs that Bob was weakening. His patience and stealth were starting to pay off, and he was about to turn up the heat.

Over the past twelve months, Dennis had carefully sown seeds of discontent about Bob among the management team. This had trickled down to the shop floor and to the sales team. As a result, people were now beginning to question Bob's ability as president.

Using divide-and-rule tactics, Dennis nurtured the discontent between sales and marketing and the production departments, and put the squeeze on Monty Fisk so he would feel vulnerable. Dennis knew that in order to survive, Monty would undoubtedly play his ace card on Bob, which would create enormous embarrassment for Bob and perhaps even a crisis. That was exactly what Dennis wanted.

## The Mind

At this point, however, since I have made a point of distinguishing between the subconscious mind and the unconscious mind, I feel I should offer a definition of them both since a lot of people erroneously use the terms interchangeably.

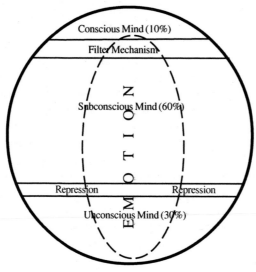

**Fig. 5:** The Mind

As you will see from the diagram above, there are in fact three areas of mind — plus the emotional component which covers all three — from which humanergy emanates.

### 1. The Conscious Mind

This is that part of the mind from which we operate with conscious awareness. It is responsible for our day-to-day cognitive activity. Most of manifest humanergy emanates from this level of mind.

# BOB

Though he had escaped birthday celebrations at work, Bob was not to be let off so lightly at home. Jean had arranged a surprise birthday party for him. He arrived home earlier than usual and found that she had invited several friends, as well as his now quite aged father, to be there. As he walked through the door they all sang "Happy Birthday," and his children rushed up to him to give him their gifts. Jean kissed him lovingly. She was younger than Bob by eight years and was an attractive, stylish woman with shoulder-length, ash-blonde hair which she usually wore down, but on this occasion she had put it up. She wore a low-cut, tightfitting white dress that revealed quite of lot of her shapely figure. Bob did his best to look pleased about the party and, once things settled down a bit, proceeded to pour champagne for a toast. "To my loving husband on his fiftieth birthday," said Jean simply. Everyone clapped and cheered.

"Thanks, everyone: let's eat," Bob said, pointing to the lavish buffet that Jean had had catered in. Once he had filled his plate, Bob made his way over to his father.

In spite of having lost a leg in the Second World War and then later becoming crippled through a car accident when Bob was just a baby, Bob's father had reached the age of seventy-nine. Though confined to a wheelchair for most of his life, he had managed to outlive Bob's mother by fifteen years. He was an extremely angry and bitter man.

"Hi, Dad. How are you doing?" Bob asked dutifully.

"Terrible," came the reply that Bob had fully expected. "The pain gets worse every year, and those stupid doctors at the VA Hospital couldn't give a damn. Not one of them! Useless bastards, all of 'em. But I don't give in, and I still work my ass off in spite of the pain. I don't quit you know, not like some people I know."

42

## 2. The Subconscious Mind

The subconscious is one level down from the conscious mind. It is that part of our mind which stores all of our learned ideas, beliefs, paradigms, attitudes, prejudices and habits as well as many of our basic needs and drives. It is programmable but once the program is in, it is very resistant to change. The content of the subconscious mind is always manifesting itself as observable behavior. It is fairly easily accessed and wide open for manipulation. Marketing people, of course, know this only too well. They know that people never buy for the reasons they think they do and that their buying decisions are always made on the basis of subconscious needs and emotional drives. Advertisers always pitch their message to appeal to the subconscious mind and to the emotions, not to the conscious, rational mind. Politicians do exactly the same.

## 3. The Unconscious Mind

This is a level which goes deeper than the subconscious. The content is much more difficult to recognize or to access. Repressed unconscious material is buried way down below the level of awareness and is seldom made manifest as observable and recognizable behavior. Our deepest fears, held shame and most painful wounds lie buried and unresolved in this part of our mind. Our most strongly held resentments remain shackled down here along with our unresolved grief and profound self-hatred. The unconscious mind is the repository of dark secrets we just can't bear to look at and base desires that we can't own. It is a dark place. The content of this part of the mind is surrounded by sophisticated defense mechanisms that keep everything hidden and deeply repressed.

Our normal approach to this material is to "let sleeping dogs lie." We are warned not to start digging, or we might get more than we bargained for. What we have failed to understand,

There was the first jab of the evening that Bob knew was inevitable and inescapable. There would be more.

"And how about you? Still at that company — what's it called?"

"Gico, Dad."

"Yes, that's it, Gico. Heard from that old partner of yours lately, the one who became a millionaire? You screwed up there, didn't you, boy? Shouldn't have left. You might have been a millionaire by now too."

"I didn't exactly leave, Dad, and I'm not doing so bad anyway. Does this make me look poor?" asked Bob, pointing to the house and everything in it.

"No, but you're not a millionaire either, are you? That partner of yours is a multimillionaire, though, isn't he? Let's face it, Bobby, you both started out together as partners and you let him screw you over. Pity you're not more like your brother. Jimmy wouldn't have let that bastard squeeze him out, no siree! If it had been him and not you, I wouldn't have lost the money I put into that business to help you get going. Hard-earned cash — made by my own hands, let me tell you, even though I am in a damned wheelchair. I ended up losing my money because of you."

"Must you bring that up again, Dad? You know darn well I repaid that debt years ago."

"Yeah, so I got my money back, but I might have been a millionaire when Rick took that company public if you hadn't screwed up, just like I knew you would. Instead of which I have to rely on my pension and whatever I make by selling my woodworking."

"Screw you, Dad!" said Bob and moved away. He could feel the rage welling up in him, and he was close to tears. He hated the man and

44

however, is that this part of the mind is not inactive. It is NOT a sleeping dog. It is, in fact, a writhing serpent. It is constantly emanating energy, and its effects, though hardly recognizable and seldom, if ever, correctly understood for what causes them, are powerful indeed. The potential that such energy carries for creating all sorts of mischief in the workplace is enormous.

It is also interesting to see how these three aspects of mind are structured in layers and how both the subconscious and unconscious parts of the mind each have a built-in system of self-preservation. In particular, there is a mechanism that operates between the conscious mind and the subconscious mind that blocks and filters information flowing in both directions.

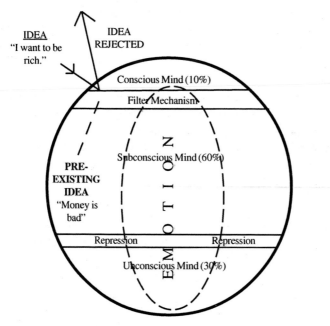

**Fig. 6:** The Filter Mechanism

wished that Jean had not invited him. Even though his mother had not been emotionally available for him during his early years, he nevertheless missed her and wished all the time that it was his father that had died of cancer instead.

When Bob was a young boy, his father would always put him down and would frequently belittle him in front of people. "Look at him," he would shout and scream. "He'll never amount to anything; no damn use to anyone! Thank God his brother Jimmy isn't like him!"

As is typical with this kind of primal wounding, and in spite of all the shaming and the beatings that inevitably followed, Bob had unconsciously spent all his boyhood and most of his adult life trying to get his father's approval and never succeeding. Every time Bob had experienced failure in his life, his thoughts would go straight to his father and the shame would be unbearable. Conversely, whenever he achieved success, no matter how good it was, he knew it would never be enough.

As a boy, Bob was athletic, wiry and strong. He was not one for team sports, but he was a good long-distance runner. He ran in a lot of races and won a fair number of trophies. His father never came to watch or support him, except once. That was when Bob was fourteen and was representing his high school in a ten-mile cross-country race. Bob came in first but only a few yards in front of the next contender. The only comment his father made was, "You nearly lost."

The only person Bob had felt really loved him and made him feel worthwhile was his grandfather. He lived close by, and from a very early age, Bob spent as many hours with him as he could. Bob's mother and father took no notice of him anyway, so they didn't care. His grandfather had a little workshop and would show Bob how to do things with bits of wood and metal. With him, Bob did not feel alone.

This filter mechanism also acts as a verification system in the sense that, if an idea occurs in the conscious mind such as "I deserve to be paid more for what I do," the filter mechanism dives down into the subconscious and unconscious parts of the mind to check whether the idea is in alignment with what already exists down there. If it finds, for example, that there is a pre-existing idea, belief system or attitudinal complex that says something like "you are not worthy of being paid a lot for what you do," or "money is bad and only bad people are rich," the idea will be rejected.

The conscious mind is comparatively weak and unable to override the subconscious mind. Therefore, in this example, the truth is that a person, who appears on the face of it to consciously want more money, really does not. He or she will, therefore, find ways to sabotage any increase in pay or remuneration. This is a very common phenomenon and, of course, is an example of negative humanergy at work.

We will explore more examples of this phenomenon in the next chapter. In the meanwhile, let me outline the nature of the four energies in both their manifest and latent forms.

### 1. Manifest Physical Energy
This kind of energy manifests as physical effort and productive output. Since it can actually be measured and quantified, it would seem more appropriate to think of it as gross energy emanating from our conscious mind. It occurs, after all, as a result of our conscious decisions. However, as our medical analogy shows, we are more than just a body.

### Latent Physical Energy
While at first blush all physical energy would seem to be gross energy made manifest, we know that subconscious

47

Though he visited his grandfather most days, there was one day that Bob, for whatever reason, decided not to visit him. That was the day his grandfather died. The neighbors had found him in his workshop, having died alone of a massive heart attack.

Bob was just five years of age, but it felt to him as if his whole world had come crashing down. He had lost the only person in the world that loved him and saw him for who he was. He had never felt so desperately alone, and yet, he could share none of his pain with his parents, least of all his father. His father had just told him not be so stupid. "Cryin' is for girls," he said and told Bob to stop crying or he would give him something to cry about.

Bob also blamed himself for the death. "If only I had gone there as usual, I might have been able to save him — or at least call an ambulance," he would always think to himself. Bob never got over the loss.

Fortunately, the guests left pretty early and, thank God, someone helped Bob's father get himself into the wheelchair-adapted mini-van that he drove. Bob had had nothing more to say to him the whole evening and was glad to see him go. He did not even say good-bye, and neither did his father.

"The mean old bastard," he said quietly to Jean as they watched him go. "I'll hate him until the day he dies, and then some."

"I'm sorry I invited him, Bob, but it felt right somehow that I should. It's been so long since you two have spoken, and after all, it is your fiftieth. But I know now that I shouldn't have. I'm sorry"

Bob turned and looked at his wife. She looked alluring in her low- cut dress, and whereas normally he would have been quick to seize the moment, he felt no desire for her tonight. "I've got to go to bed," he said. "I am so desperately tired." With that, and with his head held low, he went upstairs.

mental and emotional factors come into play at every turn and can dramatically effect our willingness to do all that is required of us in terms of productive output. So will our beliefs and our core values, many of which reside in our subconscious and even unconscious minds. Subtle energy, therefore, is also a factor with actual measurable productive output and cannot be ignored.

## 2. Manifest Mental Energy

Mental energy can also manifest as measurable behavior and ways of being. We recognize in people such things as intelligence, creative flair, practical problem-solving skills, good communication skills and so on, most of which are made manifest in practical results of some kind. Even attitudes can be made manifest through behavior.

Sophisticated tests and assessment instruments abound in the corporate environment and are designed to identify and quantify such forms of mental energy as IQ, thinking style, learning style, social skills, communication style, leadership ability, attitudes and so on. Probably the best known is the Myers Briggs instrument.

Many of these testing instruments lead on to suggest ways in which such manifest energy can be channelled in the "right" direction. Seminars, workshops and training programs that attempt to do just that are the staple fare in the area of Human Resource Development.

### Latent Mental Energy

Though the more sophisticated tests referred to above may hint at some aspects of this kind of latent energy, for the most part it remains well hidden. It certainly will not be apparent at an interview! And yet it is an energy that drives

49

Jean knew him well enough to know that something was desperately wrong, so for the first time in her life she left the house just as it was and immediately followed him upstairs to bed. She knew that he needed her.

Bob ended his fiftieth birthday in the arms of his wife, crying uncontrollably for most of the night. And he didn't know why.

# Meg

Meg couldn't get Monty off her mind. He had scared her that day — much more than she realized at the time. She really felt that he had it in for her, even though she did her job more or less perfectly. She was a perfectionist about everything, but with Monty it counted for nothing. Whatever she did, it was not enough for him. Thank God that the workers cared for her and that she was able to put her energy into taking care of them.

Meg collected Caroline from school and went straight home. Immediately after cooking them both a light meal, she crashed.

# Mrs. Harper

Gwen Harper was one of those women who you might think had been born with energy-sensing antennae. She could not only register emotional tension between people three blocks away but would have a pretty good sense of what it might be about. Not that she was psychic. The kind of sensitivity she had came from being brought up in a house where one or both parents are not only alcoholic but violent rage-a-holics as well. To survive and to stay out of trouble for as long as possible, Gwen had had to develop an ultrasensitive awareness of where the next emotional outburst might come from and to recognize the warning signs instantly.

and controls each and every one of us. It is the place from which — for better or worse — all our actions spring. This energy emanates from both the subconscious and unconscious parts of our mind. It is composed of our <u>subconscious</u> needs, drives, thoughts, ideas, beliefs, attitudes and values.

### 3. Manifest Emotional Energy
A good working definition of an emotion is "a thought attached to a feeling." Emotion is also "energy in motion."

Feeling gives energy to ideas such as loyalty, team spirit, and desire to succeed. Without the feeling component those would be empty ideas with little energy attached to them. Feelings don't come from the prefrontal cortex; they come from the more ancient part of the brain known as the limbic system. But feelings carry enormous energy. They are the source of all our motivations.

Emotional energy shows up in observable ways in such qualities as a person's desire to achieve, need for recognition, passion about the work, ambition, competitive spirit, commitment, loyalty, team spirit and so on. Programs that foster these qualities of mind have been very popular in recent years.

Daniel Goleman, in his book *Emotional Intelligence*, showed that manifest emotional energy can be nurtured and developed as a highly valuable resource. This movement, begun by Goleman, has done a great deal to bring awareness of how important emotional energy flow really is. Many corporations are now training people to become more emotionally intelligent — helping them to

She also learned to say very little or, better still, to say nothing about what she saw or heard going on around her. The safest strategy was to act as if nothing had happened and be as invisible as possible.

She continued to effect that strategy at Gico, much as she had done in her own marriage, most probably. Her husband had died ten years ago, and her four children were all grown and married. She lived alone with her two cats.

Gwen was fully aware of all the ongoing tensions between Bob Pearson and Dennis Barker, and she saw through all the subtle and not-so-subtle power plays that each of them indulged in. But they didn't know that, of course. She had perfected the art of being invisible and giving the impression of being totally unaware of what was happening around her. She never spoke of what she observed and never offered advice. She had strong opinions, of course, but she always kept them to herself.

She also knew a lot about Bob Pearson's background by virtue of the fact that her old schoolfriend, Barbara Fields, had ended up marrying Rick Tanner. Gwen had maintained that connection and had therefore, through Barbara, heard all about the drama that occurred when Rick forced Bob Pearson out of their partnership. Naturally, she saw it all through Barbara Tanner's eyes at the time and never did meet Bob. Neither had she ever let on to Bob when he joined the firm that she was an acquaintance of the Tanners or that she knew what had happened. She almost lost it, though, when that e-mail came in from Rick on Bob's birthday. She came close to letting out a gasp when she saw it, but Bob was too self-absorbed to notice.

Her awareness of what was going on was not limited to the executive floor. She somehow managed to stay in tune with the emotional energy field of the entire firm. She had a good ear for the gossip that is common between secretaries and assistants, and she was able to make correct intuitive connections with only the smallest tidbits of information. She was also able to confirm her intuitions by going to

understand, accept and manage their emotions and to use them as a valuable resource.

However, as you might have noticed in the diagram on page 45, emotions exist more in the subconscious and the unconscious parts of our mind and are therefore beyond awareness. Men, especially, are very cut off from their feelings, having been taught from an early age to deny them or suppress them. Even when emotions do come into awareness, many of us push them back down. For this reason, I think it is fair to say that most subtle emotional energy is latent.

### Latent Emotional Energy

Latent emotional energy that emanates from just below the level of awareness has a great deal of potential to either enhance or impede the energy flow as it attaches to ideas, thoughts, beliefs. While manifest emotional humanergy shows up in positive forms such as enthusiasm, loyalty, commitment and pride in one's work, latent emotional energy is usually negative in nature. It will typically manifest as anger, greed, fear-based manipulation, false pride, prejudice, need to control, need to be right, need for approval, etc.

Subtle emotional energy of this nature has its origins in emotional wounds and core-negative beliefs that lie deep in the unconscious mind. It is therefore potentially explosive and will almost certainly be acted out in some way in the work situation.

### Feelings and Ideas Must Align

Like mental humanergy, emotional humanergy is subject to the filter mechanism between the subconscious and the conscious minds. Just as an idea that forms in the conscious

the personnel files to which, as the president's personal assistant, she had unfettered access.

Gwen came from a large family. She was the second of six children: four boys and two girls. Her older brother, 3 years her senior, treated her just like her father treated her Mother. Her father was of the firm opinion that women didn't matter much and didn't require a higher education because they would become either a nurse, a schoolteacher, or a secretary. When her father sold his business for 14.4 million dollars, the boys got equal shares; the two girls got nothing. Not a penny. Gwen was furious but could never confront her father. He was just too powerful, and she was terrified of him.

Her mother was a kind and sweet soul with a weak body. She was always sick in bed or crawling around feeling terrible. It saddened Gwen to see her father be so demanding of her mother in spite of the fact that she was weak, exhausted, and ill. It was as if he didn't even notice. In order to protect her mother, Gwen began to work around the house at a very early age and to take care of the other children. Her only sister was the baby in the family, so basically Gwen became mother and maid in that household. The boys were not expected to help out in the house in any way, and her father expected to be looked after all the time. Her early life was a real struggle, and when she got pregnant in her late teens, her father disowned her, saying she brought shame on the family even though she married the man prior to the child's being born.

She despised Monty Fisk. She knew of his prior connection with Bob, of course, and understood only too well how he had set it up with the search firm to recruit Bob Pearson in order to sabotage Dennis Barker's chances of becoming president.

Not that Gwen Harper had much time for Dennis Barker either, let it be said, but she had been extremely attached and loyal to Charles Bottomly, the other candidate, who had died within a year of retiring.

mind has to align with pre-existing ideas in the subconscious mind in order to be accepted, so must the emotion attached to the idea also be in alignment. Otherwise the idea will be kicked out.

That's because *feelings always win out over ideas.* Average people, especially men, think that their thoughts will always win out over feelings, and they imagine that if they try hard, do the work and think positively, success will naturally follow. It will not. There are no exceptions to this rule.

For example, suppose a person is consciously trying to create success in his working life. If the feeling quality attached to that idea in his subconscious mind is a positive, warm feeling, then success is likely to occur. If, on the other hand, there is a subconscious fear attached to the idea, then success will not occur, no matter how much he works at it.

### Fear of Success
Fear of success is a very common pattern. It can form in response to a number of past experiences but a very common one is where, prior to becoming successful, a child's father was attentive and loving to his wife and child.

The more successful the father became, the less attentive he became towards his family, and his neglect may have led to a breakup. The child would probably have formed an association between his father's increasing success and both his own and his mother's pain. That would have led to his forming a subconscious core-negative belief that *success equals pain and always leads to unhappiness.*

55

She really had wanted him to get the job, and she firmly believed that he would be alive today had he done so. In her mind, it was the disappointment that had killed him, and to a large extent, she blamed Monty Fisk.

It was also not escaping her keen attention that Dennis Barker was maneuvering himself to wrest back from Bob Pearson the job that Dennis had always felt was his, by aggravating and capitalizing upon Bob's current state of depression. She could read Dennis like a book.

Though she had been loyal to Charles Bottomly and was disappointed that Bob Pearson was appointed, she nevertheless liked Bob from the beginning. She very soon became willing to defend and protect him from all the covert negative energy that was projected towards him, and she wasn't going to stop now. Neither was she going to let Dennis Barker hurt Bob. She was an extremely good and loyal secretary to Bob, but she was sensitive to his feelings too and worried about him when he felt down. It was all she could do not to mother him.

Besides having this uncanny ability to know everything that was going on without appearing to do so, and to remain more or less invisible, she also had a very strong caretaker streak. If she saw someone being treated unfairly in any way, she would feel their pain intensely and would work in very subtle ways to make sure that some restitution occurred.

In her mind, she saw the people who worked at Gico as her family, and she felt a deep need to be responsible for them, just as she had been with her own siblings.

This need to be a "silent" caretaker and anonymous benefactor fitted in with her need to be invisible and to keep everything she knew inside and hidden. However, it led her to exist very much in her own inner world, separate from other people. Though on the surface she was quite sociable, no one could get close to her.

## Blocking Success — Without Awareness

A person with that kind of unconscious fear will, if they begin to be successful, find ways to unconsciously sabotage themselves. They will then create ways to cover it up by blocking the energy flow in their department so that success becomes less likely.

Such an energy pattern might be very difficult to spot and even more difficult to remedy by orthodox methods. Even the person with the fear will be totally unaware of it and will be unable to understand why they cannot create success. They will blame everyone around them or find fault with the system which they can only imagine is the cause of their apparent failure.

## Humanergy Attached to Our Wounds

Latent emotional energy attached to whatever has been stuffed, suppressed, buried, denied and repressed deep down in the *unconscious* part of our mind is even more dangerous. It is the energy attached to our wounds, our resentments, our deeply felt pain, and/or our shame or guilt and it is the strongest subtle energy that we possess. It has enormous power over us and can be extremely destructive — or enormously creative. It all depends upon how we access it and learn how to harness it.

Up to now, handling this kind of energy has been considered to be the province of skilled therapists. So, naturally, it has never been addressed in the context of human resource management.

## The Myth

To imagine that it is only the mentally unstable who possess this kind of latent emotional energy, and that ordinary

57

The shadow side of Gwen Harper's ability to "take care" of people without drawing attention to herself was that she was equally adept at secretly sabotaging those she didn't like and about whom she had strong judgments. She was very self-righteous and was always quite sure she knew what was best.

Her current concern, however, was with Meg Smith. She really liked Meg and felt very drawn to her, seeing a lot of herself in her perhaps. She had heard a lot about Meg and her wilder days but had developed a lot of respect for how Meg had pulled herself up by her bootstraps and made a decent life for herself when she might easily have gone the other way. Not that Gwen was above taking some credit for this herself. After all, it was she who had pulled a lot of strings to get Meg her job at Gico.

It was during her abusive first marriage that Meg had met Rick Tanner and had a brief affair with him. His wife Barbara never knew about it, so Gwen, too, would have remained ignorant of that had Rick not called Gwen and asked if she could get Meg a job at Gico. He had said that she was a friend and just wanted to do her a favor, but Gwen could smell the guilt and the deception. She knew what a womanizer Rick was and knew immediately that he had had, or was having, an affair with Meg. When Meg arrived at the interview, she was clearly pregnant, and even though Meg was married, Gwen had no doubt whatsoever in her own mind that the baby was Rick's.

At the time she was very angry with Meg for having the affair with her friend's husband and judged her severely, but she knew Rick well enough to know that it would have been mostly his fault. As time went by, she dropped her judgment and began to really like Meg. She saw a lot of herself there. She recognized Meg as a good mother to Caroline and a very good supervisor at work, especially in the way that she took good care of her workers and was willing to defend them against that horrible tyrant and woman hater, Monty Fisk.

people are free of it, is to subscribe to a myth The truth is that every single person coming to work on a Monday morning, from the highest-paid to the lowest-paid worker, arrives with a huge amount of unconscious latent emotional baggage. Attached to that baggage is an equally huge amount of subtle energy. And this energy is not stable, inactive or contained. Just like radioactive material in an ordinary barrel not lined with lead, it is radiating energy all the time and there is no way to control it. And, unless you have a very special tool to detect it, you don't even know that it's there. That's how subtle it is. And that's how dangerous it is in terms of its potential to block energy flow at every level up the chain.

If you have been reading the story on the opposite page, you will know what I mean. Each of the characters in the story brings their unconscious baggage to work with them and, often in quite destructive ways, acts it out in the workplace.

## 4. Manifest Spiritual Energy

Spiritual energy is made manifest not so much by what people do with this kind of energy, but by their way of being. Whereas mental and emotional energies flow from the mind and ego and are coarse, spiritual energy flows from the soul and is the finest of all energies. *(Note:* Love energy flowing from the heart is spiritual energy, not emotional energy.)

People who emanate spiritual energy show up as loving, compassionate, caring and open to seeing the world in terms of the underlying truth of what is rather than the way it seems. They don't teach truth so much as they live it. They demonstrate truth. They are inner directed, quiet

She had been carefully tracking how Monty had turned on Meg and blocked her promotion on a number of occasions. Gwen had listened to Monty telling Bob Pearson how Meg needed strong handling and that she might be trouble if Bob moved her into another department and gave her a promotion. Bob always gave in to Monty, and Gwen Harper knew why, of course — which is why she decided that she would intervene as soon as the opportunity presented itself.

# BOB

Gwen Harper took the call. "Mrs. Harper, this is Jean Pearson. Would you please tell everyone who needs to know that Mr. Pearson will not be in today? I think he might have picked up a bit of food poisoning at the party we threw for him last night — not real serious, I don't think — so he should be in tomorrow. Would you do that for me? Thanks. 'Bye."

Bob threw a glance at Jean and wondered whether he would indeed by able to pull himself together sufficiently to return to work in the morning. He had never called in sick in his life, and for him to take a day off was quite unusual and totally out of character. *(That fact had not been lost on Mrs. Harper, either.)* He looked, and felt, terrible.

Jean had gotten the kids off to school, and now they were alone. She had been worried about him for months, but he would never talk about his feelings and always brushed her aside whenever she asked him if he was worried about anything.

"What's going on, Bob?" she asked. "You've never cried like that for as long as I've known you. You were like a scared little boy last night in bed. You need to talk about it, Bob, or you'll crack up."

Bob just stared vacantly into the fireplace. He would not look at Jean. Finally he said, "I'm scared of losing it all, Jean. I feel that I am in quicksand, and I am being sucked down."

60

and centered. They do what is necessary in the world out of a sense of what is right — always referencing the core values that come not from external sources but from within themselves. They come from integrity.

Jesus was the finest example of all, but there have been many others. Gandhi demonstrated the power of spiritual energy to overcome the military, economic and diplomatic power of Great Britain in the liberation of India. Nelson Mandela demonstrated the same quality in South Africa and avoided what could have been an inevitable blood bath. Martin Luther King was another. You can no doubt add examples of your own.

### Latent Spiritual Energy
Spiritual energy is available to more than just a few special people. Whether we manifest it in the way we have just described or not, it is inherently latent in every one of us, for deep down we know the truth of who we are.

We know that in our pure essence we are the energy of Love and that we are indivisibly connected to the Divine and one with it. Whether we find that divine connection through Jesus, Buddha, Krishna or Allah, through communing with nature, or by direct means such as meditation, makes no real difference. We are all spiritual beings and we are essentially spiritually intelligent.

## Spiritual Intelligence
This will be covered in more depth in Part Two, but it seems appropriate to say a few things about it here in relation to the subject of latent spiritual energy.

61

"By what, Bob?" Jean asked.

"I don't know."

"Are things getting really difficult at work again? Is that it? Is Dennis putting pressure on you?" Jean waited for a response that was long in coming.

"Yes, but that's not it. I've had work troubles like this before, and I can handle Dennis Barker. I know he wants my job, but I'm always one step ahead of him."

"Then what is it, Bob? Is it us?"

"No," said Bob quickly, looking up at her. "It's not our relationship. I love you, and we're fine."

Jean had run out of questions and could only look at him and observe how pathetic and childlike he seemed at this moment.

" I feel like I am dying," he said.

"What do you mean?" Jean cried.

"Oh, don't panic — it's not my health. I'm fine physically. No, I'm not going to die — I'm just saying that this feels like death to me."

With that, Bob buried his head in his hands and then, after a few moments, got up and hurried to their bedroom. She knew he needed to cry alone.

# Dennis

After Gwen Harper had called and told him that Bob Pearson was sick and wouldn't be in, Dennis allowed himself a wry smile. He

First of all, let me make it clear that spiritual intelligence has nothing to do with religion or spirituality as such, and it is not a belief system. It is a "knowingness" that seems to be part of who we are and is almost akin to instinct. Except for people who have been so severely wounded that their soul has been fractured into a thousand pieces, everyone has it.

Ancient people were in tune with spiritual energy, and they knew how to use their spiritual intelligence. They understood it. They were able to access it, and it gave meaning to their lives. Indigenous people today still have this connection in a way that modern, industrial people can hardly fathom. We seem to have had it programmed out of us.

## Connecting
Yet modern man yearns for that kind of connection, and many are now beginning to tune in to their own spiritual intelligence. They are making connections with latent spiritual energy in all sorts of ways that are tremendously empowering. Sometimes these ways take some rather bizarre and extreme forms which inevitably invite criticism and scorn, but it doesn't matter. The important thing is that people of all types are beginning to tap into reserves of subtle spiritual energy within themselves and are using the practical aspects of it in their everyday lives.

## Corroborating
As we pointed out in Chapter One, physicists have recently come along with the theoretical underpinning to corroborate everything that is already contained in our own spiritual intelligence, so it can no longer be dismissed as mere emotional clap-trap or new-age wu-wu. It's hard to argue with mathematics and with the finest minds in the world.

knew that Bob was close to a breakdown and sensed that this might be his best opportunity yet to oust Bob and take over his job.

From an early age, Dennis had been driven to be number one. In his eyes, coming second was the same as losing, so winning was everything to him. With that kind of mind-set, the ends always justified the means, and Dennis had followed that path all his life. So long as he won in the end, he had no qualms about how he did it.

But he was as smart a man as he was ruthless. He was extremely patient, knowing how to bide his time and wait for the right moment to strike. He also had perfected the art of the act and always gave the impression of being everything that he was not.

He had studied and mastered Neuro-Linguistic Programming (NLP). This is a form of awake hypnosis that was originally designed as a powerful healing modality for reprogramming the subconscious mind. However, because it was a form of hypnosis that was performed while the person was totally conscious, it could also be performed surreptitiously.

This made NLP very attractive to people who wanted to manipulate others at the subconscious level without their being aware of it. Salesmen, obviously, thought of it as a blessing and Dennis was no exception. He became extremely adept at using it to control others. It was largely through his ability to control and manipulate people without their knowing, and to be how he thought others wanted him to be, that he advanced his career in sales in general and at Gico in particular.

Dennis was born into a family of Irish descent. Both sets of grandparents had immigrated during the potato famine of 1910 and had settled in Boston. Dennis's parents were very poor and his father was a drinker. Dennis was the fifth child of eight and always felt that he had to fight for mere survival.

## Who's Using It?

It is probably true to say that the best corporate leaders have always had the ability to use spiritual intelligence, whether they did so consciously or unconsciously. However, many more CEOs are now realizing the value in doing so and are consciously and purposely moving in that direction. There are a few notable examples where some high profile companies have fully integrated the notion of spiritual intelligence into their normal everyday operations.

But on the whole, awareness of spiritual intelligence and how it can be used in the daily operation of a company to good effect is still very low, and the resistance to it is extremely high. This is absolutely to be expected, of course, because to accept the idea of using spiritual intelligence as a major resource in the daily operation of the company demands a paradigm shift of quite major proportions.

Sociologist Thomas Kuhn described three stages in the process of a new paradigm becoming accepted.

**1.** Total resistance to and ridicule of those proposing it.
**2.** Attempting to explain it by referencing it back to the previous paradigm using the same language and concepts.
**3.** Acceptance of its being completely self-evident.

> [Returning to our earlier analogy between medical science and managerial science, it is inevitable that high-level corporate managers will do what the top people in the medical profession have done. They will resist the idea of spiritual intelligence and fail to see its value in the workplace *(Stage One)*. They will join their counterparts in the medical profession who, even today, refuse to let go of their old reductionist paradigm and rudely dismiss mind/body/spirit approaches to medicine, and they will likely dismiss spiritual intellingence out of hand.

He had always felt deeply ashamed of his family and vowed that he wasn't going to end up like his father, a broken man. Out of all the children, he was the one who took himself off to night school with the sole aim of lifting himself out of the lifestyle he despised and to escape the family he was so terribly ashamed of. He was intelligent and a fast learner. He had succeeded in becoming a well-educated engineer, but he soon was drawn towards the sales side of the business. His Irish charm and a gift for quick thinking and fast talking made him a natural for sales. He had joined Gico, Inc., some ten years previously as a technical salesman and had steadily risen through the ranks to become vice president at the age of thirty-six.

From very early on, Dennis had set his sights on the top job and was extremely disappointed and angry when he didn't get it. Not that he showed it, of course. That wasn't his style. He appeared to take it in his stride and to support the board's choice, but inside he was seething. He vowed that he would do whatever he had to do to wrest that job, at the earliest opportunity, from whomever held it at the time. Dennis would not be happy until he was number one at Gico, Inc. But he was never one to attack directly. Dennis knew that if he was too overt in trying to unseat the president, that Bob would fight him very hard and might well fire him.

No, he knew that the best way to get Bob Pearson was through Monty Fisk. With Bob away at least for a day and probably more than that, this was a good time to sow some seeds and to begin unsettling Monty to the point where Monty might feel it necessary to play his survival card with Bob Pearson. Dennis picked up the phone and asked his secretary to put a call through to Monty Fisk.

# Gwen Harper

Gwen Harper was also sharp enough to see an opportunity when it presented itself. She put a call through to one of the secretarial staff

This is absolutely indicative of the defensive nature of the sub-conscious mind, to which I have already alluded. The resistance the subconscious mind throws up against a new paradigm is directly proportional to the emotional investment in the existing paradigm. Having gone through many years of very costly training and amassed a reputation as an expert in the field, a doctor has an extremely high level of emotional investment in the paradigm that not only defines the nature of his or her work but who he or she is. No wonder then that the resistance is overwhelming. We can only feel compassion for doctors as they struggle to resolve the inner conflict that arises because of it. Corporate managers are in exactly the same position.]

This book is positioned clearly on the side of the new paradigm that recognizes corporations as complex energy systems that need to be understood and managed from that standpoint. Its purpose is to open and encourage that conversation and to introduce ways of capitalizing on that understanding, especially that of humanergy in general and spiritual intelligence in particular *(Stage Two)*.

We shall return in Parts Three and Four to the specific ways that spiritual intelligence can be used in the daily functioning of the corporation, no matter what size it might be. In the meantime, let us continue our examination of how humanergy operates to impede the flow of energy within the corporation.

in the production department she trusted well enough to know that it wouldn't get to Monty Fisk's personal secretary, to the effect that Mrs. Harper would like to have a word with Meg Smith. A few minutes later, her phone rang.

"Hello, Mrs. Harper, this is Meg Smith from production. I was told that you wanted to speak with me."

"That's right, Meg," Gwen replied. "I would like a word with you if you have a moment. Actually, I would prefer that it be off the premises. Would you care to have lunch with me today?"

"Of course," said Meg. "That would be nice. I get my lunch break around one o'clock. Is that OK? "

Gwen told Meg to meet her at 1:15 at a particular restaurant and to not let anyone, especially Mr. Fisk, know that she was having lunch with Gwen Harper. Meg arrived on time, and as soon as they had ordered, Gwen opened the conversation.

"Meg, I've been noticing that you haven't been yourself lately. You look very tired and stressed out. I'm worried about you. What's going on?"

"Oh, nothing really," Meg replied, a little taken aback by Gwen's directness. She had been wondering all morning why Gwen had quite uncharacteristically suggested a lunchtime meeting. "I'm just a little tired trying to be a mom as well as a full-time career woman. But I'm fine really."

"Is Mr. Fisk still coming down hard on you?" asked Gwen, thinking that she had to come to the point quickly. "I'm hearing on the grapevine that he is making things really tough for you. Is that right?"

Tears immediately began coming to Meg's eyes. She could feel Gwen's concern for her and immediately connected with her compassion. Even

# 5
# Humanergy Dynamics

Having outlined manifest and latent forms of humanergy in the previous chapter, let's now look more closely at how they originate in people and how they operate dynamically to either enhance or impede energy flow in the corporation.

**Note:** Since managerial science has largely mastered the more manifest aspects of humanergy, my focus from this point on will be on the latent forms of each kind of humanergy — mental, emotional and spiritual. (Latent physical energy is basically an amalgam of the other three and will no longer be considered separately.)

## Creative Thought
It is now generally understood that thoughts and ideas are creative in the sense that they produce actual effects in the world. Also, that the more emotional energy there is attached to them, the more likely it is that they will create a corresponding effect out there in the world. This is the basis of all goal-setting strategies, motivational systems, and many other methods of optimizing human performance.

though she was an executive secretary, Gwen could just as easily be your mother in moments like this.

Meg dropped her guard and began to relate to Gwen all that had been going on between her and Monty and how it was wearing her down and undermining her self-esteem. She told Gwen how Monty had threatened her the day before and how he had wielded his power over her. She just couldn't understand why he hated her so much, especially since in the early days he had seemed to like her and had supported her.

For her part, Gwen was acutely aware that her own dislike for Monty Fisk and her desire to protect Meg from his overbearing behavior were becoming even more intense.

"Please don't say anything to Mr. Pearson, Mrs. Harper," Meg pleaded. "If it this gets back to Monty, my life won't be worth living."

"Don't worry, Meg. I won't. But I won't let Monty get away with anything either. If he threatens you again, I want you to let me know. I cannot stand injustice, and even more so, I hate the idea of men trying to use their strength to overpower women. I won't let it happen to you, Meg." Meg felt relieved and cared for. It was a good feeling.

When Gwen Harper got back to the office, she checked messages and found none from the Pearsons. She thought it was strange, but took advantage of the time and the freedom to go into the personnel files. She was hoping she could find something on Monty Fisk that would weaken his hold over Bob Pearson.

She was in something of a quandary though, because she sensed that Dennis was also getting ready to pounce on Monty Fisk for reasons of his own. She knew he knew about Bob and Monty and had been waiting for an opportunity to expose the whole situation in order to embarrass Bob, so she was not anxious to provide him with any ammunition. Dennis could care less about Meg Smith.

## Think and Grow Rich

No one is more associated with this idea than Napoleon Hill, author of *Think and Grow Rich*. That book was written in the 1930's and has sold millions of copies worldwide. It was he who said, **"Whatever you can conceive, you can achieve."** Napoleon Hill was the first person to popularize this most basic of metaphysical ideas — that thoughts create reality. The more emotional energy there is attached to the thought, the more powerful it is and the more likely that it will manifest in form.

## You'll See It When You Believe It

So, yes, thoughts and ideas are very creative. Beliefs, which can be described as a set of highly crystallized ideas and thoughts, are even more so — especially if there is a strong emotional charge attached to them. Beliefs act like internal gyroscopes and literally create our lives day by day. As Dr. Wayne Dyer has said, "You'll see it when you believe it." It became the title of one of his books.

## Core Beliefs

Most of the ideas we have buried in our subconscious minds were imparted to us from our parents, at an age when we were highly suggestible to them and other significant "god-like" people. These ideas and beliefs then became firmly embedded in our subconscious mind as *core* beliefs. Some of those beliefs were positive and affirming. These become our *core-positive beliefs*. Others were negative and restricting. These became our *core-negative beliefs*. Both of them are running our lives, whether we know it or not.

Core-negative beliefs are always unconscious. They are the reasons why affirmations rarely work. As we saw in the diagram on page 45, a subconscious idea will always take precedence over a conscious one, no matter how much you think you want what you are affirming.

71

Gwen thought long and hard and then made a fateful decision that would ultimately change the fortunes of Gico, Inc. She called Rick Tanner and told him about Bob.

# Bob

Bob slept virtually all that day, all through the night and into the next morning. Jean was happy about that. She knew that nothing heals like an extended sleep, and she left him alone as much as she could, except to bring him water and some snack food which he hardly touched. She saw it as the direct result of stress and feared that it might have been a nervous breakdown. It did not, however, occur to her that it might be his dark night of the soul.

Bob, on the other hand, had a sense of it being just that, though he would never have used that language to describe it. Yes, stress was a factor, but what was happening to him was caused by something far more profound. Some part of himself was boiling up and wanting to surface, but he didn't understand what it was or how he should react. Bob was scared.

About mid-morning a FedEx packet arrived. Jean looked at it but didn't open it before taking it up to Bob, who was now sitting up and feeling a little better. He opened it and found that it contained a book. He looked to see who had sent it, but it had been dispatched by a bookstore addressed to Mr. Robert Pearson. There was no note, no invoice, nothing.

The title of the book intrigued him: *RADICAL Forgiveness: Making Room for the Miracle*. He had never heard of the author nor even any of those who had endorsed the book. Shrugging his shoulders, he put it down on his bedside cabinet and went back to sleep.

## Scripting

Have you never wondered why children from rich and successful families tend to be able to produce financial prosperity and material success virtually without trying, whereas children from poor families have to really struggle to make it? It is simply a matter of subconscious scripting. People from rich families have a subconscious script (set of core-positive beliefs) that says that money is good, it is easy to attract, and prosperity is to be expected. So that's what they create. The opposite is true of people from poor backgrounds.

Core-positive beliefs tend to support people in getting or achieving what they want, whereas core negative beliefs create the opposite effect. Here are some examples.

## Core-Positive Beliefs

a) Typical core-**positive** beliefs to do with our personal self might include

> *"I am lovable and likeable."*
> *"I am a powerful person."*
> *"I am a person worthy of being given . . ."*
> *"I deserve . . . "*
> *"I always create success."*
> *"I am good at my job."*
> *"I can do anything I set my mind to."*
> *"Money comes to me easily."*

b) Typical core-**positive** beliefs to do with how we see life might be

> *"Life is good."*
> *"People are inherently good."*
> *"My company values me."*
> *"I am well-rewarded for what I do."*
> *"I can trust life."*
> *"People won't steal from me."*

73

Once more, Jean left him alone but kept on wondering who had sent Bob that book — and why that one? Not that he didn't need a miracle right now! "He could really use one," she thought. After lunch that day, she decided she must talk with Dennis Barker and Gwen Harper and give them some idea when Bob might be returning. She didn't want to say too much, but there was no hiding that something quite serious was happening. She told them that Bob was suffering from nervous exhaustion and that she thought he needed to take at least a week off, if not two. On the other hand, he would probably be available for consultation from home in the next day or two. She only talked to Mrs. Harper, but she knew that the message would get to everyone who needed to know. She went back up to Bob about two hours later just to check on him and found him sitting up and almost devouring the book. He seemed to have gotten some of his life back all of a sudden.

"Jean, whoever sent this book must have known something. It's really quite extraordinary, and even though it's not my normal way of thinking, it's striking chords in me left and right."

"What does it say?" asked Jean, marvelling at how Bob had really perked up.

"Hard to explain really, but it is starting to ring some bells. I'm even beginning to see what might be happening to me," he said almost to himself. "Let me finish reading this chapter, and then, rather than trying to explain it, I'll let you read the first chapter. Then you'll see what I mean."

Once more Jean left him alone, but this time it was different. Something good was happening, she felt. But who had sent him that book? She went through a list in her own mind, but no one really popped out. Who might have cared enough to do it and then to remain anonymous?

c) Typical core-**positive** beliefs to do with how we see ourselves and life from a spiritual perspective might be

*"I am a beautiful child of God."*
*"I am protected and guided at all times."*
*"Everything happens for a reason."*
*"Everything is in Divine Order."*
*"Love is all there is, and I am Love."*
*"Things always work out for the best."*

## Core-Negative Beliefs

a) Typical core-**negative** beliefs to do with our personal self might include,

*"I am unlovable."*
*"I am inferior because I am black."*
*"I will always be discriminated against."*
*"It is not OK for me to be powerful."*
*"I am not worthy of anything."*
*"I don't deserve . . ."*
*"I am a failure."*
*"I am not good at anything."*
*"Everything I touch goes bad."*
*"They just don't appreciate me."*
*"I am invisible."*
*"My company undervalues me."*
*"I am never paid well for what I do."*
*"Even my own mother/father hates me."*
*"I hate my mother/father."*
*"I have to be perfect to get approval."*
*"I have to be right."*
*"There is never enough . . . "*
*"To be loved, I have to be who I am not."*
*"Everyone else's needs are more important than mine."*
*"I will never amount to anything."*
*"If I become successful, I will become like my father."*

75

# Dennis

As soon as he got the news from Gwen Harper that Bob Pearson was having what Dennis interpreted as a nervous breakdown and wouldn't be back any time soon, he decided to make his move. He called an emergency meeting between the sales department and the production department to discuss what should be done in the light of the latest sales figures. He made it sound as though he and Bob had planned the meeting beforehand for this date, and that even though he couldn't be present, Bob nevertheless had given his blessing for the meeting to go ahead as planned. Gwen Harper, of course, knew otherwise but kept silent and remained as invisible as possible. She would, however, take very careful minutes of the meeting. Dennis did not know that she knew so much about what was going on; he had always been somewhat oblivious with regard to her.

Monty Fisk vehemently protested about having the meeting at all, contending that the meeting was all one-sided since Mr. Pearson was really the person who directed the production side of the business, and he was not there to provide the strategic point of view. Of course, Monty knew he was being set up by Dennis and that Dennis was out to get him this time. He knew his position was precarious without Bob Pearson there. His protestations were in vain, however, and the meeting was fixed for later that same day.

Dennis had made a point of quietly appointing two or three loud-mouthed people in the sales department whom he could rely on to spike the meeting with strong complaints about how production could never adequately service the contracts that the sales force created, and that, as a result, there were a lot of complaints from customers and many lost sales. He encouraged them to be as vociferous in their criticism of Monty Fisk as they liked and to point out, in no uncertain manner, how he refused to modernize and seemed unable to bring the company into the twenty-first century. That way, Dennis could stay above the fray, appearing to be only chairing the meeting, and, as usual, looking good.

b) Typical core-**negative** beliefs about how we see life might
include,

> *"Life is inherently a struggle."*
> *"People are inherently bad."*
> *"All men are like my father."*
> *"All women are like my mother."*
> *"Rich people are crooks"*
> *"You cannot trust any man/woman."*
> *"Black/White people are no good."*
> *"Gays are an abomination."*
> *"I cannot trust life."*
> *"You can't trust anyone."*
> *"This is a dog-eat-dog world."*
> *"It's survival of the fittest."*

c) Typical core-**negative** beliefs to do with how we see life from a
spiritual perspective might be

> *"I am a no-good sinner."*
> *"I deserve to be punished."*
> *"I am being punished."*
> *"This is my bad karma; I earned this."*
> *"Evil lurks everywhere."*
> *"I created this terrible circumstance."*
> *"If I am spiritual, I should be able to heal myself."*
> *"Since I haven't been able to heal myself, I am a bad
> person and a spiritual failure."*

## Parental Influence

Core-positive beliefs tend to be predominant in people raised by
warm, supportive parents who affirmed their uniqueness and particular identity. There is generally a high correlation between high
self-esteem and predominance of positive core beliefs over negative
ones, especially those concerning the self.

77

Dennis began amicably, saying that the meeting was to be open and exploratory, without finger pointing on either side. The aim was to see why the figures were down even though the economy was up and to have some discussion about ways of improving performance. But he knew he could depend on his sales staff to make trouble, since most of them had had it in for the production staff for many years anyway. He knew they would be calling for blood.

It turned ugly very quickly, and the finger pointing started. And they all pointed at Monty Fisk. Monty knew then that, without Bob Pearson there, he was going to be hung, drawn, and quartered by everyone, including, it has to be said, by some of his own staff who, seeing the way the wind was blowing, chose to support the winning side. He was cornered and he knew it. He tried to rescue the situation by referring to plans that were in the works to improve production performance, a good many of which were already on Bob Pearson's desk awaiting his approval. He asked Dennis to adjourn the meeting pending the review of those plans. Knowing that the damage was already done, Dennis graciously agreed and brought the meeting to a close but not before an agreed statement of outcome was ratified that deplored the current situation and recognized the need for drastic action on the part of the production side to modernize and improve all systems as a matter of urgency. Nobody actually said as much, but the inference was that Monty was the problem and should be replaced.

It was a bad day for Monty Fisk. Gwen Harper couldn't help feeling sorry for him in spite of her own dislike. She could feel his loneliness and desperation and despised Dennis for setting Monty up the way he had. Meg, when she heard, felt much the same. Dennis, on the other hand, gloated. He had had a good day.

## Empathic Failure

Core-negative beliefs tend to be predominant in people whose parents consistently failed to connect empathically with them. Empathic failure runs the whole gamut from severe physical and emotional abuse to simply wanting the child to be other than who he or she is.

We tend to think of abuse as being overtly physical or emotional, but empathic failure can be subtle, unconscious and in most cases quite unintentional. Indeed, children from seemingly very good families may grow up with core-negative beliefs simply because they were not really seen for who they truly were, and they grew up thinking that they were not OK.

## Withholding Love As Empathic Failure

Many parents discipline their children, or try to mold them, by withholding love whenever they fail to conform to the parents' idea of how the child should be. This prolonged withholding of love, which tends to be the discipline of choice among middle and upper class people, in contrast to lower class people who tend to use corporal punishment more, is extremely wounding to the psyche and constitutes a profound empathic failure. It results in a whole complex of core-negative beliefs that get buried deep in the unconscious mind. But, as we have noted previously, such unconscious material is highly toxic and carries enormous destructive energy.

## I Am Not OK

Psychotherapist Lawrence LeShan, author of *Cancer as a Turning Point,* discovered in his research into the emotional causation of cancer that all cancer patients have in common the same core-negative belief.

*"If I show up as who I am, no one will love me. Therefore, in order to be loved, I have to be someone other than myself."*

79

# Bob

Later that evening, Bob reluctantly relinquished the book to Jean, but only so she could read the first chapter, he was quick to point out. He was already two-thirds of the way through and wanted to finish it as soon as Jean had had a chance to read some of it. However, by the time Jean had read just a few pages, he had once again fallen into a deep, but now apparently restful sleep which was to last the whole night.

So Jean kept on reading and, like Bob, found the book to be both enlightening and at the same time disturbing. She was able to see how it related to both their lives. It started to give meaning to a number of things that had happened in their lives which, up until that moment, had seemed to both Bob and Jean, totally random and without any real meaning. According to this book, everything that happens has meaning and purpose and nothing is an accident.

To Jean, this was mind-blowing stuff. As she read on, she began to see how Bob had a pattern of creating failure over and over in his life, and that this latest episode was simply another repeat of the same thing. She also began to realize that the purpose of this breakdown was to heal something deep within himself that had caused him to keep failing virtually every five years.

Her eyes became heavy and soon she was lying beside her husband in as deep a sleep as he. But even as they slept, something was happening within them both.

Bob was awake early, at more or less his usual time. He went downstairs to make some coffee and took the book with him. By seven o'clock, he had finished the book. He went downstairs to his office, turned on the computer, and went straight to the Web site, www.radicalforgiveness.com. He logged into the online forgiveness worksheet tutorial, ready to try the process that was supposed to

80

This is clearly a very toxic belief that, in the end, shows up symptomatically in the physical world — in this case, the body. It would also show up in the way the person acted in their personal relationships at home and at work: inauthentic, false, manipulative and codependent.

## We Create Our Reality

Each one of these core beliefs generates the energy that shapes and directs the energy field in which it is contained. These beliefs then interact with other complex energy patterns in the person's overall energy field and with those in the outer world that resonate naturally with it. This interaction produces corresponding effects in the outer world. In other words, whatever a person believes will show up as their reality. Whereas we used to say "I'll believe it when I see it," we are now coming to realize that we are closer to how Dr. Wayne Dyer saw things a decade or so ago if we say, as he did, *"I'll see it when I believe it!"*

**Fig. 7:** Projection of Reality

81

work almost instantaneously. But whom to forgive? He remembered the e-mail that had come only a couple of days ago. Well, he thought, why NOT Rick Tanner? Bob still had pain around that event even though it was many years ago. He would like to be free of it, for sure. This form of forgiveness — radical forgiveness — was so different from traditional forgiveness that it really bore no relation to anything he had hitherto understood as forgiveness. So perhaps it might work with Rick Tanner. "Unlike traditional forgiveness, it is supposed to work almost instantaneously, so I'll soon find out," he reasoned to himself.

Bob spent the next hour and a half doing the online worksheet around Rick and the betrayal that he felt had occurred. The worksheet required that he write the story of what happened, to be the "victim" fully and to feel the feelings associated with the situation. Bob certainly was able to feel the anger and hurt, and he could feel the pain in his chest just like he had when that e-mail had arrived from Rick. But as he progressed through the worksheet, the pain in his chest subsided and the anger seemed to dissipate. By the end of it, Bob felt more peaceful than he had in years. The pain was gone. Something had shifted in him and yet he didn't know what had shifted or why. It was a weird feeling. In response to a bunch of statements, he'd answered "willing," "open," "skeptical," or "unwilling" *(to accept),* but had not done much more than that. "How could that have changed things so drastically?" he thought to himself, just as Jean walked slowly down the stairs and came towards him.

"It's OK, Honey," he said quietly. "It's over. I'm on the mend. But, you know, I don't mean that in the sense of it being business as usual. I have changed, and it feels good. I don't know what it means, but the whole world looks different to me now."

"I think I know what you mean," she whispered as she held him to her in a tender embrace. "I read a lot of the book myself last night as you slept. It's going to change both our lives."

## A New Paradigm

The very idea that human beings could actually create situations and circumstances with their thoughts was, until quite recently, unthinkable. People who said that they could do such things were considered either evil or insane. In the Middle Ages such people were hounded, tortured and killed, mostly by being burned at the stake.

More recently and even up to this day, people who talk about creating reality with their thoughts (other than in sports and motivational programs which have tended to embrace the idea), are viewed as wacky, odd and decidedly New Age. They are certainly not to be taken seriously.

### Newtonian Physics and the Cartesian Viewpoint

For hundreds of years the idea that thoughts create reality has run counter to everything that we held to be self-evidently true. It went against all our long-held scientific paradigms based largely on Newtonian physics and on the mechanistic, reductionist viewpoint bequeathed to us by French mathematician and philosopher Rene Descartes almost 400 years ago. He viewed the world and even the human body itself as simply a machine that could be understood by breaking it down to its smallest, most basic constituent parts. He was adamant that there was no such thing as spirit. Emotions and mental processes were regarded as the products of brain activity.

(Many people in medical science still see it this way. The late Carl Sagan, author and presenter of the TV series, *The Cosmos,* was adamant that everything to do with mind could be explained in terms of brain function alone.)

Descartes and his followers maintained that what couldn't be measured and/or perceived with the five senses didn't exist. This set the stage for nearly four centuries of closed scientific/rational thinking that has severely limited our ways of seeing the world and ourselves

83

"It's already changed mine," said Bob. "This morning, I went online and did a forgiveness worksheet on Rick Tanner. I'm not saying I like him any more than I did before, but the pain has gone. The betrayal — well, strangely enough, it doesn't seem like a betrayal any more. It seems like there was a higher purpose in it somehow; it's hard to explain."

"You don't have to," she replied. "I think I understand. After breakfast, I would like to do one for myself. There's a few people I need to forgive too."

Later that morning, Bob put in a call to Gwen Harper. "Hello, Gwen, I'll be in around two o'clock this afternoon. Would you cancel that meeting I'm supposed to be going to in New York on Friday of next week and book a flight to Atlanta instead for both Jean and me? We'll need to get there before midday. We'll be there the whole weekend, so book us a flight back early on Monday morning. Thanks. See you at two."

Gwen Harper was dumbfounded. He sounded more up and alive than she'd heard him sound in years. Something had happened in the last couple of days, but she couldn't imagine what it was. She put in a call to Monty Fisk but decided to forget to tell Dennis. She set to work preparing the minutes of the previous day's meeting so they would be ready on Bob's desk by the time he got in.

Bob came in right on time and went straight to his office. He read Mrs. Harper's report and immediately called her in. "Tell me what happened — and I want the whole story."

Bob listened carefully and fully understood what had occurred. He recognized it as an obvious ploy, not only to directly challenge his leadership, but to force Monty Fisk to come to Bob and call in the favor he always felt he was owed, thereby bringing it to everyone's attention. This was no surprise to Bob since he had always known that Dennis would make a grab for the top job if the opportunity ever

within it. Our current medical paradigm is still pretty much wedded to that old paradigm. It, too, is essentially mechanistic and reductionist and still based almost entirely in Newtonian physics. Only as it moves gingerly into the realm of energy medicine does it begin to align itself with quantum theory — a lag of at least seventy-five years. That's how long it has been since quantum mechanics overturned the prevailing view of reality as defined by Isaac Newton.

## Theoretical Proof Exists

Quantum physicists have given us the theories and the mathematics to prove that reality is, in fact, our own consciousness projected outward, so that idea is no longer theoretically in contention . It is not yet easy to apply to everyday living, but as we have already pointed out, more and more people are beginning to observe it operating in their own lives.

## Discovering Our Subconscious Beliefs

The problem is that the core-negative beliefs that effectively create our reality are, by virtue of the fact that they are the ones we have repressed and buried in our unconscious mind, totally out of our awareness. Generally, we have no idea what they are. However, they can be inferred.

The easiest way to know what our core beliefs are is to work backwards. If we look at what is repeatedly showing up in our lives, we will discover what our beliefs are. It really is that simple — once we know that we are creating it. Most people still don't know that they are.

## Example:

> In my early adult years, I was a school teacher. In my first teaching job, I taught both Sociology and Creative Design. I was given a beautiful workshop/studio in which to teach, and it was equipped with all-new machines and hand tools.

cropped up and that Dennis had absolutely no scruples about doing so — no matter who got hurt in the process.

Surprisingly, Bob felt neither angry, threatened nor upset. In fact he almost felt like laughing. He also found himself feeling sorry for Dennis that he should be so driven to carry out these kinds of schemes, hurting himself as well as others in the process. He made a few strategic calls and then called Dennis on the intercom.

"Hi, Dennis. I'm back. Would you come to my office please, right away?"

Dennis went immediately into shock and, for the first time in his life, was speechless. Gwen Harper had not told him that Bob was coming in today, and Dennis had convinced himself that it would be many days before Bob would return. To hear his voice strong and forceful on the phone was totally unnerving. He straightened his tie, took a deep breath and then made his way to Bob's office.

"Quite a stunt you pulled yesterday, Dennis," said Bob, leaning back in his chair, looking Dennis straight in the eye. "Well, it has cost you your job, and it might even have cost you your career."

Dennis said nothing, but went very pale. He just stared back at Bob in disbelief. This was not the Bob Pearson he knew.

"I have nothing against you personally, Dennis," Bob went on. "I only wish we could have worked together as a team, but for as long as I have known you, you have sought to create divisions within the firm purely to satisfy your own ambitions. You have soured relations between sales and production purely with the intent of undermining my position so you could jump into my shoes."

Dennis was about to protest his innocence, but Bob put up his hand and stopped him. "Did you really think I didn't know?" said Bob. "I

The teacher next door to me had the exact same workshop, tools and equipment. Once day he came to me and said, "Colin, you must lose a lot of tools," to which I replied, "No, I don't believe I have lost a single tool. Why do you say that?"

"Because I notice that you leave your room open for the children to come in whenever they want. Your cupboards are left open, and the kids are free to take the tools out to use even when you are not there. I, on the other hand, always lock my door whenever I leave, I lock the tools away in boxes and I put them in a cupboard which I also lock, and I still lose tools! So I don't see how you can be so lax and not lose tools."

At the time, I had no explanation for him, though I couldn't help noticing the very large key ring absolutely loaded with keys that he held in his hand. All I could do was shrug my shoulders and say, "Well, I don't." He went off swinging his keys and scratching his head.

Of course, now I realize what was going on. He had a core-negative belief that *"people will always steal from me."* I did not. His belief manifested as his reality and the kids stole from him.

**Resonance and The Law of Attraction**
Beliefs are literally packets of energy and they carry their own specific resonance. Other people who happen to be in the same morphogenetic field as the person carrying a particular belief will tend to pick up those vibrations and come into resonance with that belief, especially if there is a lot of feeling attached to it.

Typically, and quite unconsciously, they will do things that support the person's belief. For example, if you have a belief that you don't

have known all the way along that you would do anything to get this job away from me. You are totally transparent, Dennis.

"Because of the rifts you have caused, you have been very toxic and costly to this company, and I have grave doubts that you could ever change. I need to have people around me I can trust, Dennis, and you have given me plenty of reasons to think I can never trust you. I am therefore relieving you of your post effective immediately. We will work out a generous severance package for you in recognition of your years of service, but I need you out of here right now."

"You're firing me, Bob?" asked Dennis incredulously, leaning forward and slowly rising from chair, unwinding like a snake about to strike.

But again, Bob was ready for him. He looked Dennis right in the eyes and shot back at him. "Yes, Dennis, you're fired. I'm sorry it has to be this way, but you brought it upon yourself. But listen to me, Dennis, and hear me good. As I said just now, this could be the end of your career — but it needn't be."

Bob paused, but kept looking straight at Dennis. "So long as you leave now, quietly, without making any fuss whatsoever," he continued, "I will help you get another position by giving you a decent reference. On the other hand, if you make things difficult around here — even for a day — I will see to it that you never work in this industry again. Do I make myself clear?"

Before Dennis could say anything, Bob went on. "Oh, and by the way, Dennis, I made my relationship with Monty Fisk known to the chairman right from the very start, even the bit about Monty having tipped me off about the opening, so Monty never did have any leverage over me on that score at all. He may have thought so, just as you did, Dennis, but he really didn't. Ironic, isn't it?"

Dennis did not respond. By this time he had gone from deathly pale to deep red and purple, and he looked as if he were about to explode.

really have much of real importance to say, people will resonate with that belief and will tend to ignore you. In that way, they will teach you what your core belief is.

The children resonated with my colleague's belief and somehow overcame his elaborate security system and stole his tools. Unconsciously, they were trying to teach him what his belief was.

They had nothing to teach me in that arena, so they left my tools alone. That's not to say they didn't have other lessons to teach me. They did. Kids are great at mirroring our beliefs. They are our greatest teachers.

## Net Gain or Loss to the Corporation

At the common-sense level, we can say that if a person's overall energy field is dominated more by negative core beliefs than positive ones, it is likely that they will tend to inject negative energy into the overall corporate energy field. Conversely, people with a preponderance of core-positive beliefs will, more than likely, inject positive energy into the corporation. That is assuming, of course, that they are allowed to do so. By that I mean if a person with a preponderance of positive beliefs found himself under the control of a boss with a mind-set dominated by core-negative beliefs, the likelihood is that he would be blocked by the boss's negative energy.

Imagine, for example, what might happen if a person with an *"I can do anything"* core-positive belief comes up against a manager who, deep down, feels insecure in his job because he has an unconscious core-negative belief such as *"I will never be any good at anything, so in order to be right about that while appearing to be competent, I must create incompetent people around me to take the blame."*

The negative belief might have originated from his mother's telling him over and over again "you will never amount to anything; you're

All the veins in his neck were standing out, and his eyes blazed with rage. But he knew that Bob had him hooked and literally held his future in his hands, so he knew better than to say all that was right there in his throat.

"I would like you to have your office cleared and be gone by the end of the day tomorrow. That's all, Dennis. Thank you."

Bob had felt calm during the exchange and remained so even after Dennis had walked out of the office without saying a word. Bob felt he had done the right thing both for the company and for Dennis. Bob felt good, not so much at having gotten rid of Dennis but at having found his own power again. The weekend workshop he had booked himself into in Atlanta was going to be good for him, and he knew it.

It was now time to talk to Monty Fisk before the news of Dennis's removal got around. Bob wanted to be the one to break that news to Monty.

When he did so, Bob let Monty have his moment of triumph and to express his relief. Then he went on to make it very clear to Monty that everyone who needed to know about the past knew everything there was to know, and that Monty should not count on any favors from Bob, either now or in the future. He also put Monty on notice that the plans for modernization had better be good, or he might well be the next to go. Bob also made it clear that Monty must commit to working with the new person who would be appointed as sales and marketing vice-president, and those under him, to create synergy and cooperation or, again, face the prospect of looking for another job.

Monty left Bob's office in a total daze. He had been delighted to hear about Dennis, but was completely shaken by everything else Bob Pearson had had to say. He had never heard him be so direct and truthful, and Monty was left with no doubt as to his own vulnerability.

just like your father — a lazy good-for-nothing SOB." Such shaming input would have gone deep into his subconscious mind and
would remain there, always creating situations to prove it right.

In order to be "right" about his unconscious core belief, the manager would very likely block the positive person's energy, stifle his
or her creativity and inhibit productivity.

## Everyone Loses

This situation is not in the least bit unusual and is a good example of
how humanergy operates to the detriment of everyone. Clearly, the
manager himself loses, the employee loses and so does the corporation — big time. The net loss to the corporation in terms of energy
could be enormous.

## Acting Out the Wound

Behind every negative core belief lies a deep psychic wound. Some
even describe it as a hole in one's soul. Without awareness, our
manager would have been acting out his woundedness and lack of
self-worth caused by his mother's telling him over and over when he
was growing up that he was no good and, like his father, would
never be able to turn his hand to anything: something he had heard
so often that he came to believe it. But what a toxic belief to have!
It would have kept him small and folded over for most of his life,
always in fear that his incompetence (which he would create in order to be in alignment with his belief), would be discovered and for
which he would be, once more, shamed.

> **Note:** We must remember that such beliefs are deeply buried in
> the unconscious mind, so there is absolutely zero awareness of
> this inner conversation, and even of the belief itself. The belief
> and all the defense mechanisms surrounding it are so well-cam-
> ouflaged that no one would be in the least bit aware of what was
> really happening, least of all the person acting out the belief.

Bob had made it very clear to him that he had to shape up or face the same fate as Dennis.

# The Workshop Experience

Bob and Jean returned from Atlanta on Monday afternoon feeling great. Both of them felt revitalized and transformed by the experience. The workshop had given them and all the other participants the opportunity to go fully into their stories and to feel and express their feelings about what had happened in the past, or was happening to them now, before moving into a process of transformation around the whole thing.

Since both Rick Tanner and Dennis had brought forth betrayal issues for him, Bob told the group everything that had happened between him and those two people. But the real work began, and his transformation came about, when he began sharing first about his dad and then his grandfather. He was given total permission to feel and express his anger around his dad which he did in a way that was both cathartic and freeing. Beneath that anger he discovered a terrible sadness that emanated from way deep down in his unconscious mind. The sadness came from knowing that the approval he so desperately needed from his father would always be denied him — because his father was incapable of giving it.

Bob finally recognized that reality and came to terms with it in a way that was totally liberating for him. He came to realize that he no longer needed anyone's approval and finally gave up his boyhood need for his father's. That was incredibly empowering for him. He also reconnected with the grief he had repressed at age five, but was still there, about the loss of his grandfather and the guilt that was associated with not having been there when he died. Bob began to see how all of that was driving his life and how he himself was actually creating events in his life that replayed these events in symbolic

This is why normal conflict resolution procedures don't work. They address the outward manifestation of the issue but not the subtext underlying it. It is too well-hidden.

## None of Us Are Immune

The above example is not in any way unusual. Similar dynamics operate within all of us. After all, who can say that they don't carry one or more core-negative beliefs. Such beliefs simply arise out of the experience of life and become part of our consciousness. It is all part of being human.

## A Shared Consciousness

It's also part of being in a given culture and/or a shared consciousness based on race, class, ethnicity, income, lifestyle and many other factors that determine our beliefs, values and attitudes at any given point in time. You have to look back only a decade or two to see how dramatically they have changed, even though at the time they seemed so fixed and immutable — even worth dying for. Almost every generation has gone to war over a need to defend what we now see as indefensible ideas and beliefs. Never did any group of people go to war over a less worthy cause than the South did to defend slavery, but at the time it seemed important and right.

## Generational Pain and Racial Prejudice at Work

America is still suffering from that awful wound to its psyche. A mixture of shame and anger still festers around the issue of slavery and all that occurred in the wake of its abolition. The issue has never been adequately addressed and dealt with, so the pain gets handed on down the generations and manifests as one of the most destructive forms of humanergy — racial prejudice, bias, discrimination and skewed perceptions of the differences between people of different races. It is an ever-present reality in the workplace.

form and confirmed his beliefs about himself, especially those put there by his emotionally wounded father.

He came to see how he symbolically recreated, over and over again, his grandfather's death, which had occurred when Bob was five years old. Every five years he would create a death of some kind, actual or symbolic, that would result in shame and grief.

The pattern was that everything would go well for a while and then fall apart around the five-year mark. He saw how Rick Tanner had actually helped him sabotage that big opportunity so that he could remain "right" about the idea that "my world always falls apart after five years" and the one about his "never amounting to anything." Rick abandoned Bob just as surely as Bob's grandfather had done by dying, and he made Bob feel totally inadequate just as Bob's father had done.

Bob saw how he had been setting himself up again to fail with Gico, Inc. He was in his fifth year as president and, right on cue, everything was going downhill.

He learned that, through something he came to understand as spiritual intelligence, he had even, at some deep level — and just as he had done with Rick — 'recruited' Dennis to play the betrayal card again for him. Furthermore, that it was all purposeful in leading towards Bob's healing. In other words, Dennis didn't really do anything TO him; rather, he did it FOR him.

Upon learning this, he felt bad about firing Dennis. When he mentioned this in the workshop, he was told that the gift always flows in both directions: that it was just as much a learning experience for Dennis as it was for Bob and that everything happens the way it should. Spiritual intelligence, it seems, always keeps things in balance. Upon learning this, he was able to let that go and to know that, in any case, he had done the right thing for the company.

## The Innate Self-Healing Mechanism
However, I have an abiding belief that all living organisms will always move in the direction of self-healing — even if at first that doesn't seem to be the case. I believe that to be true for the human race as well.

As part of a training program that included a section on wood technology, I had to study the structure of living trees from the gross level right down to the microscopic. I was deeply struck by the intricate ways a tree heals itself after receiving a wound like a blow from an axe or something similar. The intelligence that was revealed as the tree set about healing itself was awesome, and the elegance of the process was enough to bring tears to my eyes. I realized then that all living organisms have the ability to heal themselves and will always endeavour to do so. This is an example of pure spiritual intelligence.

## Bringing Our Beliefs to the Light For Healing
Consequently, I believe that people will always be moved to heal their own psychic wounds, as well as the wounds of previous generations that they carry and those of a more cultural nature. What does that mean? It means bringing them to the light, i.e., to conscious awareness.

## Enormous Resistance
However, because of the fear we have about facing our core-negative beliefs and the shame associated with them, we experience a tremendous amount of subconscious resistance to the idea of allowing them to come to conscious awareness. We do everything in our power to keep them repressed.

## Where There's a Will, There's a Way
In spite of all the resistance we put up, the urge to heal is nevertheless extremely strong and will always try to find a way. So, instead

What the workshop did for Bob in the short term was to totally repro-gram his belief system around his core-negative belief that he would "never amount to anything" and to neutralize the idea that "everything falls apart after five years." Not only did this save Bob Pearson, but it saved the company and all those in it. There was no reason for the company to slide downhill any more.

With regard to his father, it was to take Bob a number of years before coming to a place where he could truly forgive him, but even quite soon after the workshop, he noticed a significant difference in how his father acted towards him. Slowly and almost imperceptibly over the next few years, their relationship became more accepting — perhaps even a bit more loving.

Strangely enough, immediately after the workshop, Bob found him-self feeling the need to reconnect with Rick Tanner. All the old anger and resentment had gone, and he really had warm feelings about Rick. Bob kept thinking how strange it was that Rick had e-mailed him on his birthday after all that time. It was almost as if this whole roller-coaster of change and incredible growth had started with that e-mail. He really felt that Rick might have been one of the most impor-tant people in his life, but didn't quite understand why. Gwen Harper, though, could probably have told him.

# Rick

The phone rang in Gwen Harper's office. Somehow she wasn't sur-prised to hear Rick Tanner's voice. "Hi Gwen. This is Rick. How are things over there these days?"

"Well, I don't know what you did, Rick Tanner, but it sure did have an effect. What did you do, you scoundrel?"

"Why?"

of facing the belief directly and allowing it to come to the surface, we find a way to do it indirectly. We unconsciously resort to acting it out symbolically in the environment.

## All the World's a Stage and We're All Players

We do this by creating an actual drama that contains the core-negative belief in symbolic form and, through the law of attraction and resonance, bring into our energy field the perfect people with whom to act it out — people who will in fact, actually bring forth the belief for us.

Again, the example of my teacher colleague enrolling the children to aquaint him with his core-level distrust of the world is an example of that principle in operation. It's as though we actually enroll these people to create a set of circumstances that symbolically contain what needs to be healed.

## The Corporation is the Perfect Theater

What better place for these symbolic healing dramas to take place than the workplace? After all, there is usually a fair number of people available for the purpose, and more importantly, you are obliged to be around them for at least some of the day, for five days a week. When your resistance comes up, you can't just walk away, any more than my colleague could walk away from the kids.

## Spiritual Intelligence in Action

Healing dramas might show up in the corporate energy field as a sudden conflict or an unpleasant situation between people or groups of people. They can be sudden flare-ups or long-term, ongoing situations that never seem to get resolved. Since this all happens way below the surface of everyday reality, and without the awareness of anyone involved, the fact that these dramas cause severe interference in the energy flow of the corporation is quite incidental and of no consequence to the players trying to heal each other.

"Well, Mr. Pearson has suddenly come alive. He's a totally different person now. He's come into his power in a way I never thought possible. He sacked Dennis Barker on the spot after finding out that Dennis had tried to undermine him while he was away. He called Monty Fisk's bluff at long last and has taken charge of the firm in a way we have never seen before. Everyone's talking about it, and frankly, everyone is really excited. They feel like they have a leader again. So, Rick, what the hell did you do?"

"I sent Bob a book."

"What book?"

"Oh, just a self-help book."

"Well, it must have been one hell of a book to create that kind of change in someone like Bob Pearson. He's not normally the kind of guy to be into self-help. He's usually so rational and practical-minded."

"It sure sounded like he needed *any* kind of help when you called me that day, Gwen. I can tell you this — he was in the dark night of his soul right then. Believe me, I know. I've been there. And when you're in that place, there's only one kind of help that's possible, Gwen, and that's spiritual help."

"Wow, you've changed, Rick Tanner. I never thought I'd hear you talking about spiritual matters. I haven't spoken with you since you asked me to get Meg Smith a job, but you seem different. What happened to you, Rick?. Was it when you and Barbara broke up?"

"Can't go into it now, Gwen. Suffice it to say, I was forced to grow up and to face myself. What I saw, I didn't like, so I set about discovering what it was about me that made me act like a jerk. I went to the same workshop that Bob went to last week, and it changed my life.

However, it matters a great deal to the corporation. That's why the phenomenon needs to be recognized for what it really is: not just a personality clash or a disagreement over some policy or just another conflict, etc., but a perfectly normal healing drama that is, in fact, spiritual intelligence in action.

## Not Seizing the Moment

When we fail to grasp the nature of what is really occurring and fail to take the necessary steps to heal the underlying energy imbalance, the opportunity to heal in that moment is lost. Unfortunately, this is nearly always the case. Our ego-driven mental/emotional intelligence overrides our spiritual intelligence, and we remain in that stuck place. Undaunted nevertheless, our incredibly patient Higher Self (that part of ourself which is our spiritual intelligence), simply waits for another opportunity to repeat the same thing in the hope that we will get it next time.

## The Corporation Pays

Often it takes many such repetitions, with each one having to become more severe than the last, simply in order to get our attention. Not infrequently, it takes some sort of breakdown to occur before we give in to it, realize what is happening and become open to healing.

A breakdown of that sort can be very expensive for a corporation. It can mean anything from a lost sale to total disaster. Look at what happened to Enron! It would be fascinating to make a study of that situation to see what negative latent humanergy was being played out amongst the key players.

## Stop the Hemorrhage

How much better for the corporation, not to mention the individual, if the energy imbalance causing the apparent problem was healed in the moment when it first occurred.

99

"How did you know that Mr. Pearson went to a workshop last week?" Gwen demanded to know.

"I have my sources," Rick replied.

"Well, don't quote me as one of your sources, Rick Tanner. I still don't trust you, you old fart. But, seriously, I am grateful for what you did for Mr. Pearson. It sure did seem to be exactly what was needed. I am impressed, Rick, really I am."

"I'm glad it did the trick, Gwen, but really, it wasn't me. I only followed my intuition. I was told what to do, and I did it. That's it."

Gwen put the phone down and had to wonder to herself how so much could change so radically in such a short time. In spite of it all she felt exhilarated.

# Bob

While at the workshop in Atlanta, Bob had been excited to learn that there was a way to bring a version of the new technology he had experienced to the entire company, through what was termed The Quantum Energy Management System. He was determined to do so. He felt that it would help to mend the rift that Dennis Barker had created between the departments, restore relationships, and reinvigorate the whole company.

He had come to understand how each and every person in the company brought their core-negative beliefs, their wounds, and their unconscious grief to work with them, just as he had done, and that people would, and do, inevitably act them out in the workplace. The Quantum Energy Management System installs some simple processes and tools into the corporate structure that help an individual or group to automatically dissolve whatever is coming up to be acted out.

# 6
# Healing Our Primal Wounds

Since most of our own wounding took place in our early child-hood at the hands of our parents, unwittingly or otherwise, it is not surprising that the urge to heal latent parental issues is extremely strong in all of us.

These primal woundings occurred at an age when we were power-less to respond or even defend ourselves against them. One option was to totally repress the feelings and the memory of the wounding Another was to split off and form a survival sub-personality, one that was designed specifically for the purpose of avoiding as far as possible any situation that might lead to more abuse. Such strate-gies employed by the sub-personalities might include people-pleas-ing, being invisible, being hyper-vigilant, shutting down emotions, avoiding reality, lying and so on.

But as we have seen, everyone has a built-in mechanism to heal these wounds, no matter how deep they reside in the unconscious mind and no matter how unaware we are of them. Our spiritual intelligence knows they are there and that they need to be healed.

We have also learned that the main method we use to heal our wounds is to unconsciously attract someone into our life who has a similar

He knew enough about Monty's background to understand now why he was giving Meg Smith such a hard time. She obviously reminded him at some deep, unconscious level of his mother. Bob determined that he would offer to send Monty to the workshop he had just attended to see if Monty's dynamic with his mother could be healed so he wouldn't keep on acting it out over and over again with people like Meg.

He also decided in that moment to offer Meg the opportunity to become the coordinator of the QEMS program. Promotion for her was well overdue, he thought, mainly due to Monty's interference. She was caring and empathetic but at the same time could be firm and effective. She was bright and everyone respected her, so she was perfect for the job. Bob immediately put a call in to Helen Barnes, the director of human resources, to confer with her about it. Helen concurred and agreed to let Monty Fisk know of their decision. Fortunately, Helen had someone in mind who could take Meg's place, so continuity would not be a problem for the production department.

# Meg

Meg left Bob's office in an absolute whirl. She'd had no idea why Mr. Pearson had sent for her. Monty had been stone-faced about it when he had relayed the message he'd received from Gwen Harper that Bob wanted to see her. She'd intuited that Monty knew what was about to happen, but he wasn't letting on, so Meg had no idea whether it was good or bad. However, when she had arrived at Gwen Harper's desk, Gwen winked at her and let Meg know by her expression that all was well as she ushered Meg into Bob's office.

Meg stood outside Bob's office looking at the pack of information he had just given her. QEMS Coordinator? What did that mean? Although Bob had tried to explain it all to her, she really had not taken it in and did not have a grasp of what she was being promoted into.

102

energy to the person who wounded us and to use them as a way to resolve the underlying issue.

## My Boss is Really My Father

It is not at all uncommon, therefore, for unresolved parental issues to surface for healing in the workplace. For example, a person might unconsciously react to their supervisor, or to anyone else in authority over them, in a childish way, because that supervisor reminds them of their father. The father might have been a tyrant, in which case the person would almost certainly have unresolved issues around him, as well as a lot of repressed rage and an unconscious need to get even.

And get even he or she will — using the supervisor as the surrogate for the father. It might come out in all sorts of ways ranging from direct hostility to covert passive aggressive behavior. Either way it will be extremely destructive to all concerned and to the corporation itself. The loss of energy to the system will be considerable.

## Unmet Need for Approval

Many parents, probably because of their own woundedness, seem to be incapable of giving unconditional acceptance to their children and no matter how hard the child tries to be what the parent wants him or her to be, it is never enough. The child constantly seeks the parent's approval but it never comes.

If the child does well at school, for instance, they are told they must do even better next year. If they get an A, then they must get an A+ next time. The core-negative belief that forms is *"I will never be enough. No matter how hard I try, it is never good enough. It's hopeless."*

[**Note:** I have never met anyone with so-called Chronic Fatigue Syndrome that had not had this life experience in an extreme

103

However, she had certainly grasped the fact that at last she would be free of Monty Fisk. She also felt very good about the fact that she would be earning quite a bit more money.

"Congratulations, my dear," purred Gwen knowingly. Since her conversation with Rick, she now knew that the events of the last few days, including Meg's promotion, were the result of her fateful decision to put that call in to Rick Tanner. Quite how it had all transpired, other than the fact that Rick had sent Bob that book, she didn't really know, but she was ready to take credit for being the one to start the whole thing. "You deserve it, Meg."

"Did you have something to do with this, Mrs. Harper?" asked Meg, recalling their lunchtime conversation only a few days back.

"Not really," replied Gwen. "If I did anything at all, it was only tangentially. No, Mr. Pearson made the decision entirely on his own and then conferred with Helen Barnes, who agreed immediately."

"What about Mr. Fisk?" Meg wondered out loud. "I wonder how he'll take it?"

"Don't worry about Monty Fisk," replied Gwen, somewhat gleefully. "Mr. Pearson had him in there a while ago, and I think he took the wind right out of Monty's sails. Monty came out of that office with his tail between his legs. I don't think he'll be giving you any more grief from now on."

Meg walked into Monty's office. "Congratulations, Meg," he told her. "I hear you're moving into the human resources department, and that it's a promotion, right?"

"That's right. They have actually created a new post for me, but as yet, I don't fully understand quite what it entails," replied Meg, quite unable to read where Monty was coming from or how he felt about the situation. It was as if they were dancing around each other, like

104

form and who did not have the corresponding core-negative belief relating to the need to be perfect.]

The unmet need for approval from one or both parents never goes
away and, in adulthood, gets acted out all the time. For example,
an executive who is so competitive and driven to be number one that
he or she is willing to sabotage colleagues in the process of getting
to the top may still be trying to win approval from his mother or
father (represented by the boss) that was always denied as a child.

### Acting Out in the Workplace
The workplace turns out to be the ideal place for any negative emotional pattern to come to the surface to be acted out. It may show up
in a myriad of forms, sometimes obvious, most often well disguised.

Such things as passive aggressive behavior, projection, negative attitudes, driven behavior, self-sabotage and many other forms of negative behavior will indicate it, but it will reveal itself most clearly in
moments of conflict and upset. These moments might occur with
other people in the company or with other departments or with policies and procedures within the company.

### Departmental Energy Patterns/ Morphogenetic Fields
You will recall from an earlier chapter that groups, as well as individuals, have their own energy fields. Such energy fields are com-
prised of group attitudes, prejudices, cultural norms, collective interests, historical precedent, agreed perceptions of their boss, group
loyalties, class consciousness and so on. Whole departments have
their own energy patterns, many of which might well conflict with
those of other departments.

For example, on the whole, you could say that, simply by virtue of
the nature of the work each of them does, creative people tend to be
averse to being restricted and financial people have a high need to

a couple of Aikido fighters, each one waiting for the other to make a move. There was a long pause.

"I'm pleased for you, Meg," Monty finally said, without meeting her eyes. "I'll miss you."

"Thanks," said Meg quietly, not knowing what else to say, and she left the room. She was quite sure, however, that her dance with Monty Fisk was not yet over, not by a long shot.

# Bob

Bob decided that he would call a meeting of the whole company the next day. He would use it to formally announce Dennis Barker's departure, introduce the idea of bringing in the Quantum Energy Management System, announce Meg's appointment as QEMS coordinator, and explain why he felt QEMS was necessary for the ongoing health of Gico, Inc.

He wanted to use the meeting to launch his new vision for the company and to, once and for all, firmly establish his leadership. When Bob walked into the meeting, he felt strong, determined and excited, better than he had felt for years.

"Good morning everyone. I don't intend to keep you long, but I have called this meeting to personally bring you up to date on what has happened in the last week or so, to share some plans with you, and to give you some assurances about our future. As you may already have heard, Dennis Barker has left the company after a successful tenure as vice president of sales and marketing, and we have retained an executive search company to find a replacement for him. In the meantime, Jim Baker has agreed to step in as acting vice-president, and I know you will give him your total support. Thank you, Jim. We are certainly

control. One might naturally expect, therefore, that the Creative Design Department would have "issues" with the Finance Department. This is not necessarily a bad thing. It is precisely that kind of natural tension that should produce optimum results. The trick, however, is to keep the energy balanced and free flowing.

## Cold Wars

If the energy becomes unbalanced, and it will if it is not monitored and corrected energetically on a regular basis, it will feed into the negative energy patterns of the people involved on both sides who will create a legitimate opportunity to act out. The energy will quickly become adversarial in nature and a "cold war" will ensue that will likely be ongoing. That "cold war" will cause an extremely negative blockage in the flow of energy within the corporation.

**Example:** I was once asked to mediate a situation in a theater company where the tension between the male creative director and the female financial director, both of whom had equal power, was causing the entire company to become totally dysfunctional. It turned out that he was acting out his issues with his mother and projecting his aggression onto his co-director, and she in turn was acting out her anger around her father. It was a recipe for complete disaster. Once they became acquainted with what was really going on, they were able to begin working together and to have respect for each other's seemingly opposing needs and limits.

## Board Room Hidden Agendas

The very same thing can happen between factions in the board room, especially when two firms that were once competitive rivals merge and board members who were once bitter enemies find themselves on the same newly-formed board.

Severe blockage of energy can and often does happen on a huge scale when two companies with dissonant energies merge. A merger

107

sorry to see Dennis go and wish to express our gratitude for his long and valuable service to this company, and we genuinely wish him well as he moves on to new horizons.

" At this time I would like to update you on the new course that I am setting for the company — not only towards greater growth and development but with a clear vision of how we should achieve that in the best possible way for all concerned. We have some exciting new plans for modernizing the production department which we will be laying before you within a couple of months and asking for your input.

"I can share with you that I recently went through a very difficult time — personally — as we all do. However, I was fortunate enough to find a program that helped me see what was going on in my life that needed to change, not only at home, but at work too.

"As I thought about my work and how this company should be run, I realized that for a company to be strong, to be powerful, to be prosperous and to make a contribution, it needs to be founded on genuine teamwork. That doesn't just mean being efficient; it means supporting each other as human beings and helping each other be the best we can be — as people. People are at their best and contributing the most when they are happy and aligned with each other, and I intend for that to be a priority from now on.

"This company has suffered from interdepartmental rivalry of a very negative nature. This has caused a lot of unhappiness. I have seen enough of the subterfuge and the use of divide-and-rule tactics, and I will not tolerate that kind of behavior any more. It caused us to leak energy — human energy — and that is waste-ful. Human energy is a basic resource that has to be used wisely, so when we leak human energy, we lose in every other way too. We lose morale; we lose productivity; we lose profitability; we lose markets.

might look good on paper and from the point of view of the numbers, but from a humanergy point of view, it can be disastrous.

## Chrysler-Benz
When Chrysler and Daimler-Benz merged, the problems of cultural dissonance between the two companies caused an enormous energy block within the new company. The company may have merged physically, but their energy fields were so different they simply couldn't merge energetically.

The humanergy of each of the entities, while perhaps reasonably balanced within its own culture, became wildly out of balance when each one tried to come into resonance with the other. It was like oil and water. They had different vibrations. There have been a number of very notable examples more recently of mergers that turned out to be disasters for the same reason.

## It Could Have Been Different
Had these firms possessed knowledge of how to gauge subtle humanergy, they either would have thought better of the merger and called it off, or they would have taken many steps both prior to, during and after to bring the humanergy of both entities into line with each other. As it was, in the absence of sensible research in this area, they made terrible mistakes and are still suffering from them. Even now, I doubt that they know how to put them right. If only they knew how easy it might be.

## Blue Tail or Red Tail?
This kind of thing can last for many years. It was way back in the 1950s when two Australian airlines merged to become QANTAS. I am told that even today, employees still retain some loyalty to the old entities and often inquire of each other "Are you a red-tail or a blue tail?" (The two airlines carried these colors on their aircraft tailplanes). According to a long-time QANTAS employee I know,

109

"The company leaks human energy when people are not happy in their work or feel frustrated. We lose energy when we fail to promote cooperation and respect for our individual fellow worker. The single most important way that this company has been leaking energy over the last few years is through the interdepartmental conflict I have just mentioned. You all know what I am talking about.

"This kind of negative rivalry has been allowed to fester in this company for too long. In fact, I would go so far as to say that it has actually been encouraged by some managers with agendas of their own. When departments feel adversarial towards each other and seek to undermine each other, everyone loses.

"I will not tolerate this kind of thing any longer, and I need everyone to be on notice that if I see or hear of anyone engaging in this kind of behavior in the future, they will be placed on written final warning immediately. That said, of course, I am aware that no one can mandate a change of attitudes through edict, and I know that change cannot be brought about by threats or fear tactics. I am therefore instituting some new policies and training programs to help us become an organization where people treat each other with mutual respect, openness and caring and where people feel valued for who they are and don't feel the need to put others down so they can feel OK.

"I want this to be a healthier place to work because the truth is that when everyone feels good about being here, and in tune with their fellow workers, they will give of their best and we will all win. To that end, I am bringing in a training company that will help us make these kinds of changes over a period of six to twelve months. Everyone in the company will be involved, including myself, of course, and all the management personnel, staff and production people. If we are going to make these changes and reap the rewards, we must all be committed to the effort.

how you answer that question can make a difference in how you get treated at work, even today.

## Wasted Energy

Whenever energy becomes obstructed and/or unbalanced in this way in any part of the system, it seriously affects the efficiency of the company and hurts the bottom line. To the extent that management theory has focused heavily on the more manifest aspects of human energy, namely that which is mostly physical and mental, to the virtual exclusion of the more latent aspects of the emotional and spiritual, it may have cost corporations millions of dollars.

"The program they will implement is called the Quantum Energy Management System: QEMS for short. As the name implies, it will help us manage our own energy and have it be in alignment with company goals. It will help us plug the leaks and maximize everyone's contribution to the flow of productive energy throughout the firm."

Moving to a flip chart, Bob continued.

"If I can just explain this a little further — there are four main types of energy running through any company. The first is information or data. The second is materials and products. The third is money and the fourth is human energy.

"When human energy is not properly channelled or is misdirected, as in our case through interdepartmental fighting, it can block the flow of these other three here, and everyone loses. If it is properly directed, it can enhance the energy flow of the other three and everyone wins.

"QEMS will help us to learn how to refine the flow of human energy not just to improve the bottom line, which it will, of course, but at the same time to make this a happier workplace for everyone.

"At the personal level, I will not be asking any of you to do anything I am not demanding of myself. I have recently taken a personal training, given by these same people, that has changed how I see my own life and how I relate to other people at home and at work. But the difference between this training and every other program I have experienced was that it gave me tools — tools that help me to get through the difficult moments and challenges that life throws at me that ordinarily would keep me stuck.

"Fortunately for us, the technology is equally applicable and helpful to groups of people, especially groups of people who work

# 7
# The Humanergy Shadow

Carl Jung, the famous Swiss psychiatrist, made a very detailed study of that bundle of negative humanergy which he referred to as our *shadow.* It is something we all possess, and it too is buried deep down in the unconscious mind.

Our shadow is the sum total of all the negative beliefs we hold about ourselves and about which we feel deeply ashamed. We are so ashamed and critical of what we hold to be true about ourselves that we do with our shadow beliefs what we do with those other core-negative beliefs: deny them, disown them and repress them. That way, we don't have to look at them or feel the pain of the shame we have attached to them. Once buried deep in the unconscious mind, they are effectively *out of mind* altogether.

(**Note:** When we **suppress** something, we have an awareness of it but tend to deny it, even to ourselves. When we **repress** something — a thought or a feeling, we do not know that it is there. It remains completely out of awareness.)

## How the Shadow is Formed
When we were growing up and looking for approval and love from those around us, most notably our parents, we soon learned which

together. So, with QEMS you will get those same tools to help you deal with problems in your own life that you would otherwise bring to work, as well as to improve your relationships at work.

"As I said, everyone will be involved, no matter where they work, because the idea is to give everyone in the company a way of working together and resolving issues that everyone understands thoroughly and can apply easily in any situation.

"In its simplest form, you might think of it as a sophisticated system of conflict resolution and prevention. It certainly is that and we shall be using it for that purpose and benefitting from it in that regard, but it is much more.

"It is, in fact, a way to create a very special form of synergy and workplace harmony such that it magnifies the productive energy of each and every individual in the company. Everyone benefits — emotionally as well as financially. I think you are going to really appreciate the results.

"I am confident that, by embracing this system, we will all come together in a wholly new way. I think it will help us, not only to recapture the same kind of family atmosphere that once prevailed at this company, where everyone cared about everyone else, but to take that idea of caring to a whole new level. I want every person in this company to feel that they belong here and that this is a place where they feel supported physically, emotionally and spiritually.

"Let me be clear about this. I am not trying to recreate the past. Neither am I indulging in sentimental nostalgia about days that were part of a bygone age. Nor am I saying that in order to have a family atmosphere we need stay the size we are now. Absolutely not. What I am talking about here is a modern, cutting-edge technique that enables us to manage our own individual

114

of our attributes won us love and approval and which did not. Out of a sense of survival we selected the most "approved-of" attributes to live from and quickly disowned the others.

### "Cool" and "Uncool" Attributes

In other words, we decided then what was "cool" and what was "uncool," and from that we created the self-image that we present to the world. The rest we cast into our shadow and repress.

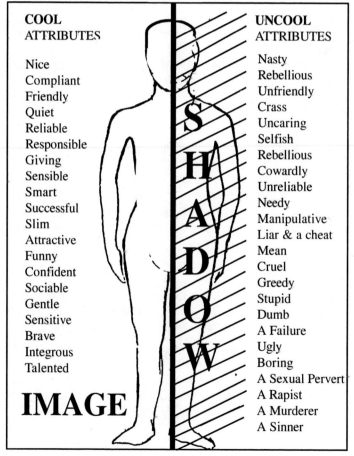

**COOL**
ATTRIBUTES

Nice
Compliant
Friendly
Quiet
Reliable
Responsible
Giving
Sensible
Smart
Successful
Slim
Attractive
Funny
Confident
Sociable
Gentle
Sensitive
Brave
Integrous
Talented

**IMAGE**

**UNCOOL**
ATTRIBUTES

Nasty
Rebellious
Unfriendly
Crass
Uncaring
Selfish
Rebellious
Cowardly
Unreliable
Needy
Manipulative
Liar & a cheat
Mean
Cruel
Greedy
Stupid
Dumb
A Failure
Ugly
Boring
A Sexual Pervert
A Rapist
A Murderer
A Sinner

**Fig. 8:** Our Divided Self

energy so that we can each give of our best for the company and, at the same time, feel personally fulfilled.

"This QEMS technology can be applied to any company whatever its size and indeed, far from keeping us the size we are, I believe it will help us to become more productive and more successful and, consequently, enable us to grow and expand in a way that has not been possible in the past.

"I want the negativity of the past to fade away as soon as possible and for us now to embrace a policy of inclusion, cooperation, sharing and mutual support. This won't happen overnight — I am well aware of that. We all have learning to do and changes to make in our attitudes, ways of thinking and ways of being. But this new technology, as long as we all embrace and agree to use it, will move us in this direction.

"As an indication of our commitment to this program, Helen Barnes and I have decided to create a new management position for someone to coordinate the whole program. I am delighted to announce that we have asked Meg Smith to be that coordinator, and she has accepted the position. Monty Fisk will miss her, I am sure, but we feel that she is perfect for the job of implementing this program and training everyone to use it to the best possible advantage.

"Meg will be taking quite a bit of training in the next week or two herself, to get thoroughly acquainted with the program and the use of the tools, and she will then be disseminating information to everyone. She will be arranging the seminars that will mark the beginning of the program and, once the program is running, will be the person we all refer to for help with using the tools as and when required. Those seminars will take place in about two months, off the premises but nearby and on the firm's time."

As we got older, we discovered, or were perhaps shamed into accepting, other things about ourselves that also appeared unacceptable. So we added these to our "uncool" list and denied them too. The seemingly more serious things for which, if discovered, we might be shamed again, we repressed totally.

## The Collective Unconscious

The collective unconscious is another term coined by Carl Jung to describe the overall energy field that contains all human beings and to which each of us has access. This large energy field contains not only our own personal shadow material but that of our parents and ancestors passed down through the generations in our genes, that of society in general and even that which is shared by all humanity — including the most archetypal of all "uncool" attributes — original sin. The guilt associated with that idea is deeply repressed.

## Active Energy

Having shifted all the "uncool" attributes into our shadow, we might imagine that they are safely buried and inactive. Nothing could be farther from the truth. There is an enormous amount of energy attached to each and every one of them, and that energy is both active and reactive.

## Mirroring

"Uncool" energy is reactive in the sense that, when we meet someone who has the very qualities we have denied and repressed in ourselves, we immediately become uncomfortable in their presence and very soon we are finding ourselves in judgment of them. This is because they are mirroring for us aspects of our own shadow. The principle here is

## *If You Spot It - You've Got It!*

Whatever it is that upsets you about the other person is what you cannot abide in yourself. The more wildly disproportionate your

117

Bob dealt with a few more items of business and then brought the meeting to a close. After he left, the room was buzzing, everyone wondering what it was all to mean for them. They hadn't totally understood what Bob was talking about, but it didn't matter. Whatever it was, it sounded good. One man from sales and marketing summed it up. "We've got Bob Pearson back, that's for sure. I don't know where we're going, but at least we're on the road again!"

# Rick

The phone rang at 7:45 A.M. That was not a time at which Rick was usually wide awake and lucid. "Hello," he mumbled into the mouthpiece, wondering who might be calling at this hour.

"Hi, Rick, this is Bob — Bob Pearson. Happy belated fiftieth birthday greetings. How are you?"

"Hey, Bob!" shouted Rick. "What's going on, old buddy?"

Bob was silent for a moment or two at the other end, and Rick wondered what might be coming next. "It was you, wasn't it?" said Bob Pearson quietly. "You sent me that book, Rick, didn't you?"

"I thought it might help, Bob. I didn't want to interfere, but I heard that you were in bad shape, so I did the only thing I knew to do. Did it help at all?"

"Rick, I'd like to take you up on your e-mail invitation to get together for lunch or something. What are you doing today?"

"I'm free. What time and where?" asked Rick.

They agreed on time and place and ended the conversation. Rick replaced the receiver and sank back under the covers, wondering

emotional reaction the more certain you can be that you are looking in the mirror.

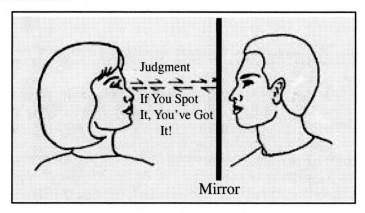

**Fig. 9:** If You Spot It - You've Got It!

This shadow humanergy is not only reactive, but *active* in the sense that, since it is a principle that a living organism will always tend to reject anything that is toxic, the urge to bring the "uncool" attribute to the surface to be accepted is strong.

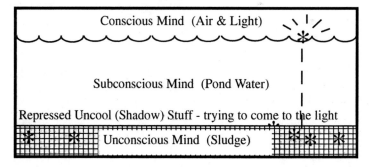

**Fig. 10:** The Innate Urge to Heal

But the idea of having our shadow material revealed, even to ourselves, is terrifying. So we expend a tremendous amount of energy

119

what the day might bring. It had been a long time since he and Bob had been together, and Rick couldn't help noticing that he was feeling apprehensive about the meeting.

When Bob hadn't answered his e-mail, Rick had virtually written off all possibility of their ever healing the relationship. But when Gwen Harper had called out of the blue and told him that Bob was close to having what she thought was a nervous breakdown, he somehow understood what Bob needed. That was because, some two years prior, Rick Tanner had gone through his dark night of the soul and knew the signs. He also knew Bob Pearson well enough to know that Bob would have buried his pain and that it would take a breakdown of sorts to bring him to his senses.

Rick's dark night of the soul had come as a consequence of his creating cancer. When he was diagnosed, he had two golf-ball-sized tumors in his right lung and a smaller one in his left. The doctors hadn't given him much of a chance, but they wanted to give him chemotherapy anyway. Rick didn't know what to do. He asked the doctors for some time to think it over. They didn't like it, but Rick always got his way. Not long after his initial diagnosis, Rick was attending a conference. He had booked late and so was having to share a room with someone who just happened to be a doctor. He had been pretty mad about having to do that, since Rick liked his own space and was used to having everything he wanted, but he'd had no choice in the matter this time. As it happened, the doctor was hardly ever in the room, so they didn't have to interact much.

During the conference Rick was in a lot of pain and having difficulty breathing. On the second night, he awoke at about 3:00 A.M. struggling to get a breath. His heart was racing, and he was sweating profusely. The noise and commotion he was making woke his roommate who, upon seeing Rick's condition, jumped out of bed and came over to Rick. "What's up, my friend?" he said. "Can I help you?"

keeping that shadow material in place — but at great cost to ourselves.

## The Beach Ball Analogy

You probably know how much energy it takes to push a beach ball under water and to keep it there. The deeper you try to push it, the more energy it takes to keep it down. Expending so much energy keeping our shadow material repressed means that we have precious little energy left for creating and maintaining health, vitality and prosperity. No wonder we are so depressed.

However, we remain ever fearful of our shadow, and we do everything we can to avoid coming to terms with it. The very act of repressing it is an avoidance strategy. But an even better way to avoid dealing with it is to project it onto someone else. Projection is the greatest avoidance strategy we have, and it is the subject of the next chapter.

All Rick could do was to point to his chest and get the words "lung cancer" out in between gasps for breath.

The conference was taking place in a retreat center a long way from any hospital, and the doctor had no drugs or other tools of his profession with him since it wasn't a medical conference. In any case, he was no longer practicing regular medicine.

He put his hands over Rick's chest and held them there. Within a few moments Rick's heart slowed down and his breathing got progressively easier. After ten minutes or so, Rick settled into a deep sleep. The doctor washed his hands under cold running water and got back into bed.

When Rick awoke the next morning, the doctor was gone. All his personal things were gone too, so obviously he wasn't coming back.

"Who was that man?" Rick thought. "And what did he do to me last night? I'm feeling so much better!" He was breathing easier and he had no pain.

He even wondered whether he had dreamed the whole thing. Then he noticed an envelope on his bedside table. When he opened it and read the note, he knew he hadn't dreamt it.

*Friend,*

*I believe your tumors may have gone, at least for now. But they will come back soon if you don't soften your heart and tear down the walls you have built up around your heart. Forgive everyone and everything, especially yourself. Love heals everything.*

*The Doc*

# 8
# Projecting Humanergy

We have learned that the kind of humanergy that is composed of latent core-negative beliefs, is stored, along with the intense emotional energy that is attached to each of these beliefs, deep down in the far reaches of the unconscious mind. Our shadow humanergy, which is that which we hate about ourselves, is also down there. We know, too, that even though all this is deeply repressed and therefore completely out of awareness, it is still radiating energy. It is like a time bomb — always ticking.

We have also learned that we all have a built-in, self-healing mechanism, which gives rise to a strong desire to bring this repressed humanergy to the light for healing. We also subconsciously enroll others to help us create situations "out there" that present opportunities to heal, symbolically, that which is "in here."

## Repression — First Line of Defense
Though this innate desire to heal is strong, the fear of bringing this repressed material to the surface is usually a good deal stronger. The thought is that the pain might be too much — too overwhelming. It creates so much resistance that we will do almost anything to stop that pain coming up. Repression, therefore, is a powerful

# Epilogue - Two Years Later

Looking back over the two years since Bob had his dark night of the soul *(he still talked about it as simply a bout of nervous exhaustion but, really, he knew better)*, he could hardly believe the changes that had taken place. Of course, Rick's having invested twenty-five million dollars into the company to facilitate the modernization had made things a lot easier, but even so, it had been an interesting two years.

The QEMS program had been introduced, and Meg Smith had certainly turned out to be a great coordinator for it. She had organized the two-day training seminars that everyone had attended in groups over a period of time and had developed a sixth sense about when people might be needing to use the tools that came with it. She kept everyone motivated to use the tools for their own personal issues and for when issues looked like they might be arising in the work situation.

Bob had made it a condition that every applicant for Dennis Barker's position had to be in total agreement with the new workplace policy with regard to the way working relationships were handled and fostered through the use of QEMS and that they were committed to their own growth.

Well, Bob had found just that kind of person in John Peterson, who had turned out to be an excellent VP of sales and marketing. John had united his team very quickly and had increased sales by 24 percent in the first year and around 15 percent in the second.

Finding common cause with Monty Fisk, he and Monty together had instituted some radical changes in how the departments worked with each other. This had led to some amazing innovations in production technology which, of course, Rick's twenty-five million had helped to implement. Nevertheless, Bob knew that the money was secondary. It was the alignment of the human energy within and between the departments that drove the changes and made them effective.

defense mechanism and, as such, we must recognize that it serves very well to protect us against overwhelming emotional pain.

Nevertheless, the need to heal is continually probing the repressed humanergy and doing all that it can to bring it to the light. We might imagine the process as a constant battle between our need to heal and our need to defend against the pain we imagine we will feel if we do indeed bring it to the light.

If it looks like the need to heal is starting to get the upper hand or even coming close to challenging the defense mechanism of repression, our psyche calls into action another powerful defense mechanism — projection.

## Projection — Second Line of Defense

Projection is our attempt to rid ourselves of a particular aspect of humanergy that has become unstable, and that just might bubble up to the surface, by projecting it onto someone (or something) else. In other words, we symbolically take it out of ourselves, push it onto someone else so we can see it "out there," and convince ourselves that we no longer have it.

Self Righteous Indignation, Anger and Judgment

You disgust me! You are such a liar and a cheat!

**Fig. 11:** Projecting Our Shadow

Three of the five people in the sales department who had aligned themselves with Dennis Barker's divide-and-rule policy, and who had been the main ones creating the trouble at that fateful meeting two years ago, had left within a very short time of the new policies being introduced. The other two came to be among the staunchest supporters of the QEMS approach and had been promoted several times. One of them, Colin Smith, was now John Peterson's director in place of Jim Baker, who also had left soon after the changes. Jim simply couldn't handle the new approach. Colin Smith had been one of those who had made it uncomfortable for Monty at that meeting, but over the last eighteen months or so they had become good friends.

Bob had sent Monty to the same workshop he had attended, and it had worked wonders for Monty in helping him to resolve his issues around his overprotective mother and to release all the core-negative beliefs about himself and life that had kept him stuck all those years. Monty and Meg Smith, who had also done the workshop as a prerequisite to becoming the QEMS Coordinator, had, in the end, developed quite a close relationship. At the first sign of any disturbance in the emotional equilibrium of his department, he would send people to Meg so she could help them with using the QEMS tools and take a keen interest in how they fared. The supervisor that took Meg's place was an older woman, but she and Monty got on very well.

About six months earlier, Monty had been offered a job as production manager of a much larger company at a considerably higher salary and had accepted it. Bob had given him a glowing testimonial, especially since he knew that the job was more suited to Monty's background and training. Monty had done well in computerizing his production system at Gico but this new firm was still fairly traditional in its approach and it would suit Monty much better. Much to Bob's surprise, Monty was there only six months before he met and subsequently married one of his staff.

Gico had gone from strength to strength and had grown into a company employing now more than a hundred people. Bob marvelled at

## Using the Law of Attraction

The way projection works is that we first use the law of attraction and resonance to pull in someone who exhibits a lot of that quality we cannot accept in ourselves. Then we criticize and judge them unmercifully for having those very same qualities, unaware of course, that they are our own. We become angry and self-righteous and will go to extraordinary lengths to make that person wrong and to punish them if possible. With the focus totally on the "bad" person "out there," the need to see what is "in here" is neatly sidestepped and avoided.

## Example:

Imagine someone who, as a young child, was caught trying to manipulate his little brother into giving up his portion of candy and, as a consequence, was severely admonished by his mother who screamed at him, "What a nasty little boy you are! How can you be so mean and devious as to cheat your own brother in this way?"

Through this experience, the older child was shamed into believing that he was not only "nasty," "devious" and "mean" but "a cheat" as well. Feeling his mother's severe disapproval, he would have immediately censored himself and would have pushed those qualities into his shadow and repressed them.

But as we have seen, repressed thoughts and feelings have a way of coming to the surface on their own to be healed. So from this point on — particularly in mature adulthood — he would always be subconsciously on the lookout for someone or something to project those things onto so as to avoid that possibility. Then he could become judgmental and hateful towards that other person as his system of defense.

127

how all the people that had been resistant to the QEMS approach from the beginning had left and been replaced by people who loved the idea and fitted right into it. Bob was quite sure that everyone in the company was now aligned with it. Who wouldn't enjoy working for a company that was committed to the happiness and the overall mental, emotional and spiritual health of its workers? The word had gotten around, and other company leaders were asking Bob what he had done to make things so different at Gico in just two years.

Gwen Harper was still his personal assistant and was as loyal as ever to him. She never would go and do a workshop, even when Bob offered to pay for her, but she got a lot out of the company seminars that Meg organized and sometimes ran. She had become much less reclusive and a whole lot less picky and judgmental in the last two years. People really liked her and always looked to her for advice. She remained the matriarch of the secretarial staff, of course, and continued to keep her ear to the ground for anything interesting.

Bob had heard on the grapevine that Dennis Barker had apparently done reasonably well for himself and was head of sales with another small company in a town a good way away. Fortunately, Bob had never been asked for a reference. One would have been due since Dennis had not made any kind of a fuss leaving Gico, as he might well have done had Bob not threatened him on that point. Bob was thankful for not having to pen a recommendation, for it would have been a difficult and delicate task.

Rick Tanner rarely came by and even then only to meet with Bob for a drink or a meal out together. He had invested his money with no strings attached and made absolutely no demands on Bob. He wanted no part in the running of the business except as a board member, and in fact, seldom ever spoke about the business. His passion lay in his work as a spiritual counselor and Radical Forgiveness coach, and, of course, he and Bob could now relate to one another on this level in a way that would have been impossible before.

## Our Enemies Are Our Teachers

Again, let's not imagine that it is only the odd one or two people who play this projection game. We all do it. Any time you find yourself criticizing someone else and getting disproportionately upset with them about it, you are projecting your own stuff. You are seeing in this other person what you dislike in yourself and have disowned. If you spot it, you've got it. That's why it is said that your enemies are your greatest teachers.

## Our Shadow Attracts Like For Healing

Now it might look as though people who challenge us, and on whom we project, come into our lives accidentally. They don't. They come to us through the law of attraction. Just as a radio station beams programs out on a certain frequency, so our shadow attributes vibrate at certain frequencies. Other people who vibrate at the same rate because they have the same shadow attributes are therefore as naturally attracted to us as a moth is to a flame.

## Automatic Healing

When we know and understand this mechanism of projection, we will realize that the other person is indeed reflecting or mirroring our disowned selves, or those parts of ourselves that we hate and which cry out to be loved and accepted. As soon as we recognize this and become **willing** to accept the person just the way they are, we automatically accept ourselves and heal that part of ourselves we had previously rejected.

## Willingness is Enough

Note the word "willing" in the previous sentence. I have found that it takes only a small amount of willingness to accept a person just the way he or she is — even a willingness to be willing is enough. And you don't have to like them or stay around them.

Rick and Bob had spent more than three hours that first day over lunch talking about the true meaning of what had occurred for each of them over the years, in the light of the philosophy given in the book Rick had sent and from what Bob had learned from the workshop he had attended. Rick had, of course, attended two of those same workshops some two years prior to Bob's doing so.

It had not been until a month or so later, and after their friendship had been totally renewed and a strong bond based on trust and mutual respect had been established, that Rick asked Bob if he could invest in Gico, Inc., to help with the modernization. There would be no favors expected, and he'd prefer that most people didn't know about it. He especially didn't want Meg Smith to know that he had anything to do with the company. He felt sure that she hated him.

Mainly through Gwen Harper, Rick had discreetly kept up with how Meg Smith was doing, and he was especially interested in Caroline. One day she and Rick ran into each other in the grocery store. To his surprise she seemed pleased to see him and was in no hurry to break away. Rick suggested they go for coffee, and she accepted. They spent some hours together catching up and talking about her new role as QEMS coordinator and his new vocation as a spiritual counselor. Naturally they found that they had a lot in common since both their careers were grounded in the same way of seeing things.

Bob was best man at their wedding six months later. Caroline was the bridesmaid. Jean Pearson organized the reception and virtually everyone from the company was there to celebrate. So was Monty Fisk.

THE END

## POSTSCRIPT

For an analysis of how the latent humanergy of each of the principal characters in this story was being acted out at work

130

## The Workplace is the Ideal Place

To get back to our man who needs someone on whom to project, the workplace is clearly the ideal place to find such a person or persons. In fact he will, through the law of attraction, bring those people to him, or will create the people and circumstances that will give him the opportunity to project these qualities. As we pointed out earlier, latent humanergy is extremely creative, and since it possesses such a strong energy, it will create the situations it needs.

You could bet good money on it that he will create the supervisor he can't trust, the assistant he won't give responsibility to and the people who will constantly act in devious way towards him. It never fails.

People who are not normally this way will find themselves inexplicably acting in a devious or untrustworthy manner towards him and inviting his anger in return. Unless they understand the dynamics of projection and the law of attraction, they will not be able to understand why they are behaving so.

Neither participant will realize that they have both come into resonance, like a couple of tuning forks. The one who needs to project his shadow part has tuned into that part of the other who has some elements of the same thing in him and, through resonance, has brought it forth. Now the person projecting is able to judge and criticize the other for what he hates in himself. It's a perfect mechanism for staying stuck — and we all do it!

## Other Likely Targets for Projection

People don't project only onto people they know personally. They frequently project onto politicians, film stars and other people who are in the public arena.

to the detriment of the company, turn to **Appendix I** on Page 203.

If you have not already read Part 1 of the book, i.e that which has been running concurrently with this story on the right hand pages, we suggest you go back now to Page Three to read the rational argument for what has been suggested in this story.

This story is also available on CD, read by the author. It can be obtained by going to the web site, www.radicalforgiveness.com and ordering it from there, or by calling 888-755-5696.

Our man here would almost certainly have an aversion to politicians and lawyers, for example, since the media are always characterizing them as devious, manipulative and well capable of cheating under almost any circumstances. Given how CEOs have fallen from grace recently and have earned vast amounts of distrust from the entire community, it is highly likely that he would project "deviousness" not only onto those already exposed but onto the CEO at the helm of his own corporation. He would reason on the basis of the law of association that his CEO had to be as devious as the rest of them.

People also project onto organizations. The IRS would be a likely candidate for our man here, as would the justice system and, more than likely, the company he works for. How much damage the latter might do depends on how senior he is, how much influence he has or what his responsibilities are.

The problem with projection is that it nearly always shows up as extreme behavior. Having attracted into his life someone, or an organization, that acts in what he interprets as a devious manner, he will tend to go ballistic. He will become extremely self-righteous and will attack the other person or the organization in ways which seem extremely exaggerated. He will pick fights with the other person and do everything he can to make life uncomfortable for him. He will accuse him of such things as "being out of integrity," or "not being up-front with me," or "going behind my back," or other terms meaning "devious."

In situations where to act openly aggressive would be against his own interests — as in attacking his boss, for example — he will do it covertly by saying bad things about the boss to others, undermining him in subtle ways and generally acting out in passive aggressive ways. Our man will not realize why he is doing this of course. This behavior is totally unconscious and, for those around him, impossible to figure out.

# The
# *Miracles*
## ―――Workshop

T his is the workshop referred to in the story as the one that Bob and Jean Pearson attended in Atlanta. The workshop is real and takes place every month in Atlanta, almost always faciitated by Colin Tipping.

This is a powerful weekend workshop for people who want expert "hands-on" assistance and guidance in moving through deeply-rooted forgiveness issues in a safe and loving space with no more than 18 people participating.

It frees one from the tyranny of the past, opens the space for miracles to occur, completely alters one's world-view and changes one's life for the better in so many different ways. A truly transformational experience!

The workshop runs from 2:00 P.M. on the Friday and ends at 6:00 P.M. on the Sunday.

For details of this and many other life-changing workshops and events, go to **www.radicalforgiveness.com.**

The book, *RADICAL Forgiveness: Making Room for the Miracle,* by Colin Tipping, can also be obtained from the same web site.

## Damage to the Corporation

Coming right back to the beginning, where we asserted that the health of any corporation depends on how well humanergy in all its forms flows through the system, we can see how humanergy that is repressed or projected can block the flow and, as a consequence, be damaging in the extreme. It is not just that there might be one person in a hundred who is liable to act out their latent energies, but that **every** person in the company is prone to do so — and definitely will do so from time to time. It is what human beings do.

So, if projecting is what human beings do as an essential part of being human, and if it is so subtle as to be hardly detectable, what, if anything, can or should we do about it? Even if it does cause a lot of energy leakage and in the end cost the corporation a lot of money, should we simply regard it as an inevitable cost of doing business?

The answer is most definitely "NO!" That's because there is a simple solution at hand that will make humanergy both easy to manage and, in its positive aspect, available as a valuable creative resource.

The solution lies in the use of that form of latent energy that has, up to now, been largely ignored; spiritual intelligence. Spiritual intelligence as a concept is discussed in Part Two and the solution to the humanergy problem that uses spiritual intelligence is discussed in Parts Three and Four.

### Note:

If you have not yet read the Gico Story, we suggest that you read it now, before going on to Part Two.

# Preface to Part Two

Before going on to explain how spiritual intelligence can be used in the workplace, I think it is important that I make clear my own view of what spiritual intelligence is, and what it is not.

In saying that, I am indicating that what follows here is only my opinion. Anything to do with spirituality — which is not the same as spiritual intelligence but is closely related to it — is open to a great deal of discussion and personal interpretation, so who is to say whether one person's opinion about it is any more correct than anyone else's? After all, spirituality deals with much that is, and probably will always remain, mysterious and unknowable. Consequently, whatever one person says about it can only be conjecture.

Not that this lack of agreement matters one jot as far as the utility of the Quantum Energy Management System is concerned. Yes, it clearly is based on the idea that there is such a thing as spiritual intelligence, and it is true that this technology calls upon it. But over the years I have found that it does not matter how skeptical people are about the underlying metaphysical assumptions of the technology. It works just the same. Belief is totally unnecessary.

## My Own Definitions

I nevertheless personally own that the definitions and concepts given here are mine, except insofar as I have been fortunate enough to have been exposed to, and therefore influenced by, the writings and sayings of some of the wisest holy men and women that have ever lived on planet Earth. If my definitions work for you, that's fine. If not, that's fine too.

Either way, it shouldn't make too much difference to the main idea presented here that there is such a thing as spiritual intelligence and it can be used as a resource, just like intellectual intelligence and emotional intelligence.

[Since I have made the point that spiritual intelligence and spirituality are related but different, let me clarify the distinction as I see it. Spiritual intelligence, like instinct, is a basic faculty that we all possess. Spirituality, on the other hand, is descriptive of how we each use and demonstrate our spiritual intelligence with a greater or lesser degree of awareness.]

## Myths Around Spirituality

However, as a prelude to the chapters that are yet to come dealing specifically with spiritual intelligence, I feel it would be helpful for me to state what I think are the myths commonly held about spirituality in general that, if not cleared up ahead of time, would lead to confusion if they were carried forward into the discussion about spiritual intelligence.

**Myth #1.** The first myth that needs to be dispelled is the idea that spirituality and religion are synonomous. They are not. We certainly can express our spiritual selves through religion, just as we can with other aspects of our consciousness, but the two things are completely distinct and separate. A religion is a very specific belief system which is so well-defined as to qualify as a doctrine or dogma.

Spirituality is not a belief system at all and requires none; it is simply our way of being and relating to everyone, and everything, around us as if we were, in some higher sense, connected.

## Taboo

The myth that spirituality is synonymous with a belief system is largely responsible for the existing taboo about discussing spirituality in the workplace. Just as we (in America) believe that church and state should always be kept separate, we have always felt, quite rightly too in my opinion, that religion should not enter into the workplace. However, in equating spirituality with religion we have made spirituality a taboo subject in the workplace as well. This is regrettable.

## No Religious Content in QEMS

The system that I am suggesting will give us the means to manage humanergy effectively, the Quantum Energy Management System (QEMS), is completely devoid of any religious content or meaning. It makes no difference whatsoever what religion, if any, the person using the technology has.

**Myth #2.** Another false idea about spirituality that needs dispelling is that spiritual people are, by definition, special, rare or unusually gifted. Popes, bishops, monks, nuns, and mystics immediately come to mind. We often think of aboriginal people as being more spiritual than the rest of us, and we imbue people like the Dalai Lama, Meyer Baba, Mother Theresa and other holy people with specialness in this regard.

Special people they may be in the way they express their spirituality in rare and perhaps difficult forms, or in the way that they live their lives, perhaps devoting a significant amount of time to spiritual practices and good works, but in essence they are no more or less spiritual than you or I. Though many people would deny it, everyone is a spiritual person. There is not a single person on the planet who is not a spiritual person. The fact is that we are all spiritual beings having a human experience.

## Work as a Meaningful Spiritual Experience

That fact means that every person who works in the corporation is a spiritual person who, like everyone else on this planet, is engaging in a spiritual journey called life. Part of that journey is coming to work every day, experiencing what it is like to exist in that place and learning how to deal with life as it presents itself at work on a day-to-day basis.

It is also about rubbing shoulders with others on their own journey, learning how to be of service to others, helping each other heal, finding a sense of purpose and meaning in life and, hopefully, a sense of fulfillment. Our interactions with each other, as we have seen already and will see again in the next chapter, will have profound spiritual meaning, even though we will, for the most part, be blissfully unaware of the fact.

## Myth 3.

Another myth I want to draw attention to is the idea that spiritual intelligence is simply part of general intelligence as we normally think of it. Clearly it is not. Neither is it measurable in the same way. IQ more or less assumes separateness of mind between one person and another while spiritual intelligence, as we have seen, is a collective phenomenon. Whereas IQ is grounded in rational thought and references the physical world and an agreed set of paradigms as to what constitutes reality based on Newtonian physics, spiritual intelligence is non-rational, non-linear and references paradigms of reality that are mysterious, non-local, metaphysical and grounded in quantum physics.

## Equality in Spiritual Intellingence

Since we are spiritual beings having a human experience, it follows that, without exception, everyone posses spiritual intelligence. I would venture to imagine too, that it is more equally spread between us all than is either intellectual intelligence or emotional intelligence.

## Intellectual Intelligence

Intellectual intelligence, as we know — because we can test it — shows a wide variability. The sophisticated instruments that measure it give us our individual intelligence quotient (IQ), which varies from the low 40s to the high 150s with the majority of the population being around the 100 mark.

## Emotional Intelligence

I would guess that the curve for emotional intelligence would look relatively flat compared to that for IQ, indicating some variability between people but on the whole showing that emotional intelligence among the population is uniformly low.

(I think most people would agree that while human beings have evolved to a very high degree of intellectual intelligence, such that, for example, we have been able to figure out how to get to the moon and back, we are still completely infantile when it comes to emotional intelligence.)

## Spiritual Intelligence

I am pretty sure that, with the exception of a few people at the lower end who have endured such terrible woundings in their lives that their souls have been virtually shattered, and a few at the upper end of the scale whom we might identify as truly holy people who have transcended physicality, everyone else would be bunched up in the middle indicating that, when it comes to spiritual intelligence, everyone has more or less the same amount.

141

In fact, it would probably be closer to the truth to say that, since it is a basic spiritual principle that we are all connected at the spiritual level, our spiritual intelligence is something that we all share collectively. Carl Jung referred to this as the **collective unconscious.** Rupert Sheldrake calls it a morphogenetic field. Quantum physicists refer to it as the Unified Field of Consciousness.

### The Evidence for Spiritual Intelligence
Rupert Sheldrake, the English biologist who created the theory of morphogenetic fields, wrote a book called *How Dogs Find Their Way Home.* He gave a number of examples of the kind we have all heard of on TV where, for example, a dog was left by its owner on one side of the country and yet turned up three months later on that same owner's doorstep on the opposite side of the country. How could the dog do it?

According to Sheldrake, the explanation lies in the idea that the dog was able to merge its consciousness into the larger energetic field of which its owner (and everyone else on the planet and, we can only assume, all dogs) was a part and then to tune into that part of the field which was specific to its owner.

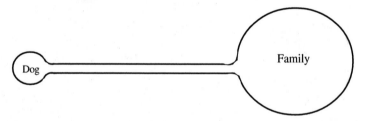

**Fig. 12:** The Family Morphogenetic Field

The dog simply started walking and, in effect, was guided by its own innate spiritual intelligence. Everything else got handled. (Exactly how everything got handled, however, remains a mystery.)

142

Sheldrake, in writing this book, has performed a great service by bringing his theory of morphogenetic fields down to something we can all relate to, because it proves that the intelligence the dog tapped into is not mental. *(No one would suggest that the dog figured out how to get there)*. Clearly it is entirely separate from the thinking function.

It also might suggest that humans, having given so much power to the rational mind, may have lost that simple ability to trust the innate spiritual intelligence that they posses or to even know that they have it. If animals like dogs and cats have it, it's a fair bet that we do too.

So what is the evidence that we still have it and that it operates continuously, even though we are unware of its doing so?

## Inferred Evidence

Spiritual intelligence manifesting as objective reality (i.e. evidence) can really only be inferred (as with Sheldrake's dog). We all can think of such instances in our own life that are just as unexplainable, and yet we find ourselves unable to write them off as pure chance or coincidence. One of the most common examples of this is what we call a 'synchronicity.'

[The word synchronicity has only recently come into general use to describe what we might have previously written off as mere coincidence but now see as an extraordinary set of circumstances that have no rational explanation yet cannot be explained away. We recognize that the odds are so long of such a thing happening in such a way or so often, that we have to preclude random chance as an explanation and conclude that a metaphysical explanation is much more likely].

Just as there is no rational explanation for a dog's finding its way home over thousands of miles, there is no sensible way to explain synchronicities other than by citing the theories that reference nonlocal reality such as morphogenetic fields or a unified field of consciousness in which normal ideas about space and time do not apply. In fact, it is only in the context of such theories that the idea of a synchronicity has any meaning at all. It is these theories that have given credence to the inference that spiritual intelligence is real.

## Subjective Evidence

Another form of evidence for spiritual intelligence is that which is essentially subjective or experienced within. These experiences, that range from psychic predictions to intuitive impressions, are so common today, and described in such terms as to seem universally much the same, that one can only assume that they are valid. Most people today are not afraid to speak about their subjective spiritual experiences. Only a few years ago, they would not have done so for fear of being ostracized.

Sometimes the two forms of evidence combine in situations where one's inner experience shows up on the outer level as objective reality. Who has not had a thought about someone far away and then two minutes later received a phone call from them? Both these forms of evidence fall short of the rigours of the standard scientific method but nevertheless provide substantial empirical evidence that spiritual intelligence is real, substantial and active in our lives.

## Summary

Here's what we know about spiritual intelligence based on the two kinds of evidence cited above.

1. Spiritual intelligence operates in nonlocal reality. This means it works outside of normal space-time parameters and is not subject to the *normal* laws of physics and everyday reality.

**2.** Spiritual intelligence is not connected to, nor a part of, other forms of intelligence which are specific to us as individuals, such as intellectual or emotional intelligence.

**3.** Spiritual intelligence is equally distributed among people.

**4.** Spiritual intelligence is not possessed by us as individuals but is something that is common to all human beings collectively, and probably to all forms of life as well.

**5.** Spiritual intelligence communicates with us — if only we listen. We are all able to receive and act upon information and practical guidance from that part of us that is connected — by spiritual intelligence — to the Unified Field.

Such communication is often described as intuition — perhaps the most basic form of spiritual intelligence that many firms have recognized as being a very legitimate form of functioning in the workplace. The most forward-looking companies are actively encouraging people to use intuition in decision making and in the creative process and to pursue training that will enhance it.

**6.** Spiritual intelligence manifests as healing energy. It can heal our bodies and minds and those of others.

[Examples of this intelligence in direct action on the physical body include Reiki, Healing Touch and other forms of spiritual healing. Examples of energy-medicine modalities that indirectly stimulate spiritual intelligence in the healing process are acupuncture, some forms of chiropractic and homeopathy.]

**7.** Spiritual intelligence reveals to us that what we see as problems, bad situations and conflicts are, in fact, opportunities for us to grow spiritually and to realize that they are not accidental at all but are created for the purpose of personal and spiritual growth.

**8.** It is our spiritual intelligence that reveals to us that the people whom we naturally regard as our enemies, and by whom we feel vicitimized, we have actually attracted into our lives for the sole purpose of providing us with an opportunity to change something in ourselves. They are therefore acting *(at the soul level)* as our teachers.

**9.** Spiritual intelligence allows us to be enrolled by others into their life dramas to act as their teachers by way of reciprocation.

**10.** Spiritual intelligence expresses itself through our physical body as feelings. When we block it, it shows up in our body as disease.

## Collective Historical Evidence

We might characterize collective historical evidence as the spiritual wisdom of sages, philosophers, mystics, poets, playwrights, holy men and spiritual leaders handed down through the ages, from ancient times to present day, in the form of spiritual writings and teachings.

There is so much of this collective historical evidence for the existence of spiritual intelligence that it is way beyond the scope of this book to even begin making reference to it. However, it is worth noting, as I have mentioned elswhere in this book, that in the last fifty years quantum physicists have more or less corroborated everything that these people have been saying for centuries. This kind of corroboration makes the evidence for spiritual intelligence overwhelming.

I will leave you, the reader, to ponder upon the books you may have read and the speakers you may have listened to and to gauge for yourself the value of this kind of evidence — for you.

Now let us turn to the specific ways in which spiritual intelligence works in the context of humanergy and how it can be used in the workplace.

# Part Two
## Spiritual Intelligence at Work

# 9
# A Win-Win Technology

T o recap Part One, we learned that there is subtle energy flowing in any corporation that has the potential to undermine or even, in extreme cases, cripple or destroy the organization. Humanergy, as we have seen, is so subtle that it is virtually undetectable. It comprises physical, emotional, mental and spiritual energy which can be active or latent, coarse or fine.

Humanergy is always operating below the level of conscious awareness, and everyone in the corporation has it —and, for better or worse, they bring it to work with them. We ended Part One with the promise that spiritual intelligence provides the key to managing humanergy.

Also in Part One, we focused on the negative mental and emotional aspects of humanergy. They are negative in their effect because they tend to emanate from the unconscious mind and are usually associated with our primal woundings, our deepest fears, guilt, shame and other repressed material.

Understandably, these negative aspects of humanergy have been considered to be not normally the province of HR managers but of skilled professionals like psychotherapists and counselors. That is exactly how it should be. **No one other than a mental healthcare professional should ever attempt to bring a person's unconscious material to the surface.** Fortunately, with the Quantum Energy Management System, it isn't in the least bit necessary to do so.

But wait! Haven't I been saying all through this book that repressed beliefs, thoughts, and feelings are the origins of harmful humanergy and that the answer is to actually bring them to the light?

**(Yes, I have.)**

Didn't I also say that these beliefs and emotions were extremely difficult to locate because they were so deeply buried and that they would resist any attempt to bring them to the light?

**(Yes, I did.)**

And haven't I said that people tend to act out their woundedness and their core-negative beliefs by creating all sorts of trouble in the workplace and poisoning important relationships by projecting their shadow onto colleagues and others in the workplace?

**(Yes, I have.)**

Well, if traditional psychotherapy is not an option, how then can we possibly begin to help someone process their mental and emotional shadow material so that it will cease creating humanergy harmful to themselves, their workmates and the corporation?

**(Good Question!)**

The great industrial efficiency guru, Dr. W. Edwards Deming, who, after having been ignored and rejected by America went to Japan, completely reorganized their industrial complex and made the Japanese the leaders in postwar production, maintained this principle: "The problem is NEVER the people. It is ALWAYS the system. Refine the system so it becomes self-correcting and error free."

## A System Refinement

Given what we now know about how individuals can dramatically influence energy flow, it would be all too easy to put all the blame on them and to do little or nothing to change the system. We might easily be tempted to say, "It's the workers who mess up the energy flow, and since the energetic interference arises from their own personal issues, there's nothing we can do about it." While that might have been true in the past, it is most certainly not true now.

We now have an answer to the problem that is both simple and elegant. The solution lies in putting into the system a process that enables people to use their own innate spiritual intelligence to bypass the mental and emotional aspects of mind and to do what is necessary, *energetically,* to dissolve the repressed material causing the interference, without having to go digging up the past or do any form of what would normally be regarded as psychotherapy.

[**Note:** It is important to add here that we are NOT talking about using QEMS with people who are mentally sick. QEMS is not a substitute for mental health treatment if such is deemed to be required, and it definitely should not be used with people who have any sort of mental illness].

Integrating QEMS tools into the organization provides precisely the kind of system adjustment and refinement that Deming was consistently calling for. Adding QEMS to the existing mix of conflict-resolution procedures and ways of dealing with grievances at the gross level gives the company the opportunity to control energy at the subtle levels as well as the more gross levels.

## Why We Need QEMS

Had we not developed into modern civilized man with all the technological benefits we have today, we might not have needed something like QEMS. Once again, let's turn to the medical analogy.

Medical science has certainly led to wonderful advances in curing disease, performing surgery and easing symptoms, but it has done so by technologically intervening in the disease process itself. The result has been to suppress and dull our own spiritual intelligence.

Not only has the use of medical science dulled our innate spiritual intelligence, it has caused us to lose the awareness that we even have this intelligence. We have actually forgotten that, by using spiritual intelligence, we can heal our own bodies and that, when it comes to healing our minds, we actually create problems, conflicts and drama out there in the world (in this case in the workplace) to serve as potential healing opportunities.

Modern technological man has become so completely detached from an awareness of this possibility that it seldom enters his head that situations are self-created for the purpose of healing something within.

**How many of us, even today, realize that it is our spiritual intelligence that brings into our life, by activating the law of attraction, the exact right person to mirror for us something that we need to love and accept in ourselves?**

As we learned in Part One, spiritual intelligence continually provides these kinds of opportunities. We also became aware of the principle that any time we find ourselves being critical or highly judgmental of someone, we are seeing in him or her those parts of ourselves that we have denied, repressed and projected onto him or her.

Have you never noticed how people keep on attracting into their lives people who tend to exhibit the same unpleasant characteristics? This is spiritual intelligence in action. It is attracting these people to act as mirrors so as to reflect back to the person what is crying out to be loved and accepted in themselves.

**QEMS technology offers a simple tool that will help people accept their shadow aspects and thereby eradicate the need for the pattern to keep recurring.**

It is very much in the company's interest to find a way to dissolve (heal) a person's need to keep bringing in people with whom he or she will inevitably "have a problem." This dynamic, created by spiritual intelligence, can be the source of much humanergy-related trouble at work.

**Using QEMS technology will enable anyone to dissolve the underlying issue and eradicate the need to attract those mirrors in the future. This in turn leads to better relationships at work and fewer instances of people coming into the workplace simply to serve as a mirror for someone.**

**Example:** There was a person at one of our workshops recently who was extremely unhappy at work because her manager was apparently making life very difficult for her and had done so for quite a number of years. This manager was constantly criticizing her and picking fault with everything she did and generally making her life a misery. "Jane" was at the point where she felt she had no option but to leave, even though to do so would have been a very bad career choice.

At the workshop she became open to the idea that the manager was there to either mirror for her something she needed to accept in herself or to give her an opportunity to dissolve a core-negative belief.

155

She returned to work on the Monday after the workshop, only to find that her manager had been promoted that very morning and would be moving to another plant.

## Simply Mysterious

The important point here is to understand that nothing was done in the workshop that would have had any physical impact on the apparent situation. This lady simply went through the process of doing a simple QEMS worksheet on the situation. That's all.

She did no more than tell the story, feel and express her true feelings around it — an essential step — and then state a certain willingness to accept, albeit with a good deal of resistance and a healthy degree of skepticism, that even though she would probably never know what it was, there might be a lesson for her somewhere in the situation.

And yet the outcome was that the whole problem went away. Against all normal odds, the situation resolved itself. Again, the only way to explain it is to say that it was spiritual intelligence in action.

Other than by reference to the concept of spiritual intelligence in action, how else can we explain the fact that we can create very complex situations, often in symbolic form, that precisely reflect and prove right some toxic core-negative belief that needs to be released?

Returning once more to the example of my teacher colleague who could not understand why he continually lost tools, it is clear that his own spiritual intelligence created those situations in which it appeared that the children had stolen his tools in order to acquaint him with his belief that no one can be trusted. At the same time, he created me to prove that he himself was the key factor. (No pun intended.)

## Slow Waking Up to the Obvious

Actually, these situations are not always so symbolic or difficult to see. They can often appear almost like actual carbon copies of the original situation, especially with personal relationships. It is amazing how often we keep repeating the same pattern over and over again. Nevertheless, we still fail to see them as self-created healing opportunities — most probably because the idea that the situation is perfect in that sense is so far from what we consider "normal" that we never even consider the possibility.

This is why we keep on creating the same kind of situations at home and at work, over and over again. If we have a wound around betrayal, for example, we will of course keep manufacturing ways to get people to betray us or let us down badly. We will constantly experience (create) people who let us down over delivery times, contracts, appointments, promotions and other promises, because we **need** those experiences to keep happening — at least until such time as we realize that our spiritual intelligence is trying to tell us something.

## A Spiritual Two-by-Four

It might take many repetitions of the same kind of situation over and over again, with each repeat being more serious than the one prior, before we begin to wake up to the truth that there is some purpose in what is happening and that we are being given an opportunity to release the pent-up energy. Very often it takes a serious health condition or an accident before we realize that something spiritually intelligent is happening and that we need to pay attention.

## The High Cost to the Corporation

These kinds of spiritual two-by-fours are almost certain to cost the corporation huge amounts of money. Continuing with our betrayal example above, imagine what it might cost the corporation to have

157

important contracts pulled at the last minute, promises and agreements reneged upon, vital deliveries delayed and so on, just to support someone's deeply held subconscious belief that they will always be betrayed.

It's difficult to conceive of people creating accidents as a way of proving themselves right, or of sabotaging themselves, but it happens. One of the big nightmares of corporate life is the money such an accident might cost in worker's compensation.

Up to now, of course, we have had virtually no awareness of the problem, no way to understand such situations and no means to prevent them from happening. Corporations have been completely at the mercy of this negative humanergy, and it has almost certainly cost them billions of dollars.

## Race-Based Negative Humanergy

Humanergy that has a set of core-negative beliefs and hate-based attitudes tied to race is particularly troublesome. Living as we do in a country that has yet to come to terms with its past relative to unequal treatment based on race, (not to mention slavery, and in the case of Native Americans, genocide), we are all carriers of that shared generational pain that cries out to be released from the collective shadow.

These issues remain a festering wound in the American psyche — for White, Red and Black people. In the absence (up to now, anyway) of any attempt at genuine reconciliation and empathic re-connection between the races, our spiritual intelligence will automatically take over. If we refuse to heal the wound, our spiritual intelligence will continually create opportunities to mirror our shadow material until we do. We must expect, therefore, to see racially inspired conflicts and lawsuits claiming unlawful discrimination arising continuously, no matter how hard we try to prevent them.

Diversity and affirmative-action programs are both well intended, but for as long as we continue trying to legislate the wound away through such policies rather than deal with the real issue, our spiritual intelligence will continue to create those kinds of opportunities.

## Bringing Racial Dissonance Into Balance

Fortunately, the Quantum Energy Management System has within its technology a way to isolate, reduce and eventually eradicate the element of race from the humanergy profile of the corporation. Not only will this help the corporation and the individual, but it will assist in reducing racial disharmony, prejudice and bigotry in society as a whole.

## OUR Highest Good — Not the Corporation's

We need to be clear that spiritual intelligence knows only what is in **our** highest interest and is totally disinterested in all other matters of a practical nature. It is, for example, completely disinterested in the well-being of any corporation we might work for. As far as our spiritual intelligence is concerned, the corporation exists only to provide the context for our learning and growing. Our spiritual intelligence might even create a situation where we take on the "wrong" job just because it might offer an opportunity to heal a particular issue.

## Taking A Proactive Approach

From the point of view of the company, the earlier that it removes the underlying (spiritual) motive for someone taking on the "wrong" job for the purpose of learning something within, the better. As I said earlier, repressed humanergy is not going to surface at the interview. It is too well hidden. This is why we suggest that all new employees be asked to make use of QEMS tools right from the start, to clear out any negative humanergy they might have brought with them. Applicants for jobs might be asked to review the technology and to say whether they would be willing to use it.

## Alcoholism and Humanergy

One of the greatest problems that HR departments face today is the high incidence of alcoholism, especially amongst those in the upper echelons of management. Employee Assistance Program (EAP) interventions deal almost exclusively with such problems and, by their discreet referrals, they keep hundreds of luxurious treatment centers all around the country in business. Everything is handled very quietly and with the utmost confidentiality, yet the cost to the corporation is enormous.

The reason that people drink and become alcoholic in the first place is that, quite simply, they are using the alcohol to medicate their repressed pain. (The same is true of other addictions too, of course, but it's alcoholism and drug abuse that costs the company the greatest amount of money.)

But the treatment only works if the pain being medicated with alcohol, drugs, sex, food or other addiction is uncovered and transformed. That seldom ever happens. In spite of the thousands of dollars the typical ten-day program costs, the person is usually back in the same place within a few weeks.

Assuming an employee chose to make use of it — especially if he or she did so before the problem became really acute — I am convinced that, with QEMS, the person with an alcohol or drug problem would stand a very high chance of healing their primal wound in a noncathartic way, transforming it energetically without the need for expensive conventional alcohol treatment programs.

With the energy pattern that was keeping the addiction in place gone, the addictive behavior would stop or at the very least become such that the EAP counselors could control it. The money this approach suggests might be saved on EA programs would probably more than cover the cost of installing QEMS in the company.

## Prevention

People would probably not become alcoholic in the first place if they had the means to deal with their emotional pain when it first began to bubble up from deep down in the unconscious mind. Rather than waiting until they need expensive treatment, what if they were given a simple tool with which to manage that first bout of emotional pain — something that would enable them to cope with it, go through it and then heal it, instead of numbing it out temporarily with a drink?

Younger employees in the company fortunate enough to have been given QEMS as a company benefit might never become alcoholics. It would be difficult to gauge how much money this might save the company over a number of years, but it would no doubt be considerable.

## Health and Humanergy

It may come as no surprise, given my tendency to use numerous medical analogies to explain how spiritual intelligence operates in the workplace, that the work which preceded the development of the Quantum Energy Management System was grounded in psychoneuroimmunology — the new medical science that studies how the four aspects of self, mind, body, emotion and spirit, interact in the causation and treatment of disease.

In 1993, my wife and I were co-founders of a nonprofit corporation called Together-We-Heal, Inc. We ran five-day retreats for people with cancer under the banner of the Georgia CancerHelp Program. Our goal was to provide an opportunity for the patients to view their "cancering" experience from an integrated mind/body/emotion/spirit perspective. (These retreats are still running.)

What we learned from this experience is that most diseases are the result of repressed humanergy. Cancer, in particular, is the result of

161

repressed rage and/or grief. We would invariably find that between five and seven years prior to the onset of the cancer, the person had suffered a severe trauma or a loss which they had not grieved or processed. They had simply repressed it.

It is also a known fact that cancer patients all tend to exhibit a marked inability to forgive and that they have developed over the years a strategy of dealing with their emotions based solely on denial and repression. They also tend to make everyone else more important than themselves. As I mentioned in Part One, they all tend to have the same core-negative belief: "If I show up as who I am, no-one will love me; therefore I have to be someone I am not."

Since traditional forgiveness takes decades to achieve, we realized that this was would be of no use for people with a year to live at the most (according to their doctors), so we had to develop a form of forgiveness that was instantaneous, easy to do and simple enough to put into a five-step process. It also had to be therapy-free since these folks had spent a lifetime avoiding facing their humanergy.

We came up with what I was later to call RADICAL Forgiveness and it proved highly successful. Why? Because it was based not on psychotherapy and ordinary forgiveness methods that use mental and emotional processes but on spiritual intelligence. I have been teaching this form of forgiveness all around the world since then.

RADICAL Forgiveness was the precursor for what has become the Quantum Energy Management System. The common element is, of course, that both use spiritual intelligence.

## Better Health Means Money Saved
If it is true that most, if not all, diseases are the result of repressed humanergy — and the science of psychoneuroimmunology is now

proving it to be so — then it follows that having a system in place that helps everyone in the corporation release toxic humanergy will lead to better mental and physical health and less illness within the workforce. This result, in turn, leads to fewer incidences of people taking time out for sickness, hospital visits, doctor's appointments and so on, not to mention increased vitality and strength of those who are at work.

# 10
# Managing Humanergy

The role of QEMS turns out to be surprisingly simple. All it needs to do is to provide a stimulus that will simply remind us of our own spiritual intelligence and to become more attuned to, and trusting of, its communication. All the tools of QEMS are designed to do just that.

As spiritual intelligence once more becomes part of our awareness, it will automatically restore the flow of positive (as opposed to negative) energy in ourselves and, by extension, to any other energy field to which we belong, including that of the corporation for which we work. It also turns out that the stimulus need only be of a subtle and gentle nature. QEMS is not invasive of privacy, requires no training or discipline — nor even belief — and is extremely easy to use. Nevertheless, it can easily transform a person's life — and a corporation too if the leadership uses it proactively as part of its strategy.

To show how a subtle technology like QEMS can bring this about, it might be helpful to return once more to our medical analogy by comparing QEMS with the particular form of energy medicine known as acupuncture.

**Acupuncture**

To an acupuncturist, disease is an obstruction of the flow of vital energy (chi) in the body. The acupuncturist restores health to mind, body and spirit by balancing the chi energy flowing through fourteen different pathways, or meridians, running vertically up and down the body. Twelve of these meridians are directly connected to specific organs in the body. Energy constantly flows up and down these pathways. When pathways become obstructed, deficient, excessive or just unbalanced, the balance between yin (female) energy and yang (male) energy is thrown off.

Yin and yang are opposite forces that, when in balance, work together. Any upset in the balance will result in dis-ease.

At certain places the meridians come very close to the surface of the body and are recognized as "acupuncture points." The practitioner restores the balance by placing fine needles in specific points, the intention being to draw off energy that is excessive, or to stimulate energy flow where it is depleted or obstructed. The effects can often be felt immediately.

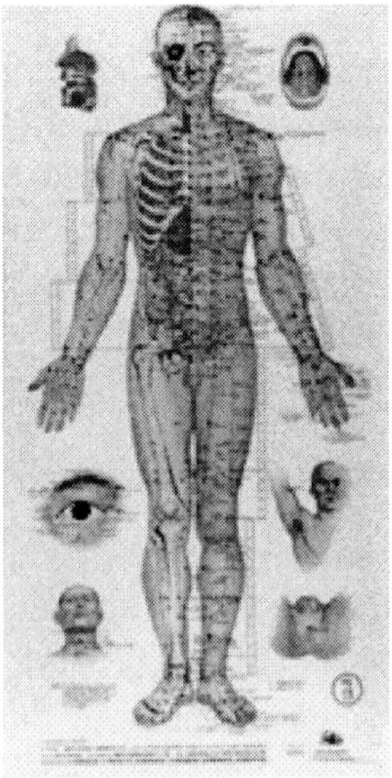

**Fig 13.** Acupuncture points on a body

## QEMS as Corporate Acupuncture

Now let's apply this analogy to a corporation. Whereas in a corporation gross energies like money, information and goods can be physically tracked and become manifest, humanergy, like chi, follows hidden pathways within the corporation.

[Note: The aforementioned meridians cannot be seen or located in the physical body. That's why medical science won't recognize their existence. The problem for doctors is that the meridians flow not in the physical body but in the etheric body — the first of five subtle bodies surrounding the physical body which, again, medical science doesn't recognize.]

We might also claim that, just as with meridians in the human body, there are certain times, certain circumstances and certain points that occur within the corporate system where humanergy might come closer to the surface than normal, presenting an opportunity for some gentle intervention to balance the flow. (**Where the acupuncturist would use a needle, we would use QEMS.**)

If the humanergy flowing in the system is yang (masculine) energy, it might manifest as conflict, heated debate or ill-considered, hurried actions or decisions that cause mistakes or even accidents. If the humanergy occurring at these moments is yin (*feminine*) energy, it might manifest as indecisiveness, passivity and emotional upset.

## Early Detection

If QEMS were in operation at the time, the situation could be observed and treated prophylactically while still in only a mildly problematic form, using QEMS tools that, just like acupuncture needles, are designed to detect imbalance in subtle energy flow in the system and to correct it easily and quickly. Without QEMS, the conflict would likely not be noticed until it became seriously inflamed and acute.

Such a situation would then seem to need intervention by the regular conflict-resolution team. But whereas, in conventional conflict resolution, the main focus would be on mediating the dispute directly and on solving the problem being presented, a QEMS facilitator would see it in quite different terms.

## We Are Never Upset For the Reason We Think

The facilitator would see the conflict as entirely purposeful in providing a sign that certain long-standing energies are coming close to the surface so that they might be balanced. The conflict would be seen as a cry for help and evidence of spiritual intelligence working its magic. He or she would see that the requirement is that the process of change be supported, NOT stopped.

He or she would then use QEMS tools (analogous to the acupuncture needles) to balance things out energetically while at the same time judiciously using, in a minimalist way, some traditional conflict- resolution methods in order to satisfy normal perceptions of what should be done in such circumstances.

The conflict would then resolve itself. Why? Because, since spiritual intelligence created the conflict in the first place in order to balance the energies, a process that QEMS tools actually achieved, the conflict would have no further use. The energy that was tied up in the conflict would then be free to move where it needed to move within the system for the greater good of all concerned — in other words, a resolution acceptable to all.

## An Energy-Related Solution

QEMS provides an energy-related solution to that part of the problem which is itself energy-related and for which normal conflict-resolution processes would not be applicable. Not only does this benefit the company by balancing energy flow, it also helps the person who manifested the conflict to improve his or her life.

168

Co-workers benefit by being around someone who seems more peaceful, balanced and happy and that in turn balances energy flow in the department. It is cumulative. Balance is restored throughout the whole system.

## QEMS is Therapy-Free

I should stress that there is no requirement that the person have any awareness of the unconscious issue being addressed through the use of QEMS tools. These tools ostensibly focus on what is being presented and require only that the person be willing to be open to the possibility that the situation is representing a learning opportunity of some sort.

It is in this sense that we assert that QEMS is "therapy-free." It does not require that the person dredge up the past or relive painful memories. The tools simply take a current situation, or one that occurred at some time in the past, to stimulate spiritual intelligence into action. The rest gets handled automatically.

The process not only has the effect of releasing the energy around that particular event (which in itself, might be seemingly quite insignificant), but all previous events related to it, including the original one to which the core-negative belief was first attached and was actually being acted out in the current situation.

## Willingness is the Key

The key ingredient that causes the energy release is the person's *willingness — even to be willing —* to entertain the possibility that, even though they might have no idea what it might be, that there is a learning opportunity contained in the situation, and that their spiritual intelligence will take care of it. It doesn't matter how skeptical the person is so long as they have just a little bit of willingness to be open to that possibility.

169

# Part Three
## The Quantum Energy Management System

# 11
# The Technology

The Quantum Energy Management System is simple, inexpensive to install, and since it is so personalized, requires very little in the way of organizational structure. Some up-front investment in initial education and training is required in order to make sure that people understand the basic ideas and the nature of the processes they will be using, but once this technology has become part of the corporate culture, it is virtually self-sustaining.

**Stage One — Initiation & Preparation**
Quantum Energy Management Consultants, Inc., or one of their certified licensed consultants, works with the company to determine how best to organize the initiation process. Clearly this will vary according to the size and complexity of the organization, but typically this will consist of:

- Orientation seminars for employees
- Training workshops for key management personnel
- Special skills training for the QEMS facilitator(s)
- Follow-up Q&A sessions prior to implementation.
- In-house coaching provided by QEMS consultants

Quantum Energy Management Consultants, Inc., will help plan and organize the meetings, seminars and trainings.

## Stage Two — Distribution of the "Q-Work" Kit

Everyone in the company is issued a small, personal QEMS kit and given formal instruction in how and when to use it to do their "Q-Work" — their own personal contribution to conflict prevention, subtle energy management and, of course, their own healing. The process is easy, non-invasive, simple and non-threatening. The kit contains the following items, often custom-made for the company:

- The On-line, Interactive "Humanergy Balancer" Instrument
- CD — "Fast Track to Radical Forgiveness"
- Pad of 50 Worksheets (Balancing "Humanergy)"
- Book — *Spiritual Intelligence at Work.*
- Book — *Quantum Healing Thru RADICAL Forgiveness*
- CD — Introduction to QEMS and Q-Work
- CD — The Gico Story, with introduction and analysis
- CD — Jill's Story, with introduction and analysis (from the Quantum Healing Thru RADICAL Forgiveness book)
- Booklets and graphical informational that explain the system and give some background to the concept of spiritual intelligence.

The three most important elements of the kit are the On-line, Interactive Humanergy Balancer, the Balancing Humanergy Worksheet, and the "Fast Track to Radical Forgiveness" CD. This CD contains two instruments:

(a) The "Satori" Balancing Process. This takes about fifteen minutes and is done while sitting in a chair with eyes closed.

(b) The 13 Steps to Radical Forgiveness Process. This takes about seven minutes, and can be done with eyes open.

The 13 Steps process is one that can be done while driving since all it requires is a "yes" response to 13 questions. There is no need to have one's eyes closed to do it. In fact, a lot of people keep the CD in the car, ready to deal with any upsetting thoughts and feelings that might come up.

At the back of this book, you will find a CD featuring the 13 Steps and a sample worksheet to photocopy and use. You will find detailed instructions for using the worksheet in Appendix II.

### The "Q-Work" Interactive On-line Humanergy Balancer

This instrument is also available to you by logging on at the web site, *www.radicalforgiveness.com*. Select "On-line Courses" from the menu and click on "QEMS Humanergy Balancer." Try it out.

The prototype version of this instrument was originally designed for people doing the Radical Forgiveness process. It was called the Radical Forgiveness worksheet tutorial. Having been available at no charge from our web site since January 2001, this instrument has proved its worth to many hundreds of people.

It was the equivalent of the regular forgiveness worksheet in my book, *Radical Forgiveness: Making Room for the Miracle,* but the online version provided an element of interactivity and involvement in the process that was different to the experience of filling in a worksheet. It was also educational in that it provided on-screen guidance, which is why we called it a tutorial.

Back in 2001, when I first created this instrument, I had another agenda besides that of providing an enhanced Radical Forgiveness experience. I saw its potential for use in a corporate program and wanted to prove its worth over a period of years before declaring it a viable tool for use in a conflict management system. Its worth has indeed been proven and I now have no hesitation in declaring its effectiveness as a constituent part of QEMS.

The Balancer might be fairly described as a "virtual worksheet," the purpose of which, as the name implies, is to help people who may be in a state of upset, to bring their energy back into balance so they can think more clearly, handle their emotions more appropriately and return to a state of relative peace. It is also designed to release the humanergy that lies behind the upset so the need to act it out subconsciously at work is decreased or eradicated altogether.

This is achieved by asking the person to give answers to a series of questions. (See Appendix II) Some of the questions require a considered written response of some length while others might require only that the person choose an option and check a box. Besides providing some interesting information that contributes to the person's self-knowledge, the worksheet helps neutralize the energy around the stressful situation (i.e. the one containing the learning opportunity) and allow the person to come to a place of peaceful resolution.

Though very sophisticated in its design, the Humanergy Balancer demands no special skill, discipline or understanding on the part of the user. It requires only that a person be willing to go through that simple, step-by-step process that will, by virtue of their willingness to do it and to trust the process, automatically neutralize those negative energy patterns. It's hard to believe that it would work, but it does. (It works because it calls upon our innate spiritual intelligence.)

## No Big Brother
This must be a completely private process and the person doing it must feel completely safe in typing in their thoughts and feelings, confident that it can never be monitored. For this reason most people use the On-line Balancer on their own home computer if they have one. Nothing is saved on the QEMS server. Once the user clicks "Finish," the worksheet is printed out and all the information is

erased forever. If the person leaves in the middle of doing the Balancer, it is set to time-out after a period of time of no activity and nothing is saved.

Another option is for the corporation to supply the same instrument on CD, especially for those who don't have a home computer. The user could then use it at work, as and when the need arose. No one would be privy to what the person writes because it is written to the CD, not to the hard drive of the computer. The CD stays with the person the whole time and is protected with passwords and the like to keep it secure. It would be theirs to use as and when they wished.

## Using the Q-Work Tools

Any time a person becomes upset, he or she might be asked to take some time out and go somewhere quiet to either listen to the 13 Steps CD or to do a Humanergy Balancer Worksheet. He or she would also be encouraged to use the On-line Humanergy Balancer at home.

## Time Taken Must Be Honored

The process might take the person anywhere from five to forty-five minutes depending on the nature of the upset and which of the Q-Work tools are selected. It is understood, however, that whatever time is genuinely necessary to do the process is honored and allowed. If cover is needed, the supervisor must provide it. However, if there were doubt about the genuine need and a suspicion that the person might be malingering, the supervisor would consult with the QEMS facilitator, who would then talk to the person.

## Outside QEMS Coaching Available

In addition to any in-house, professional, independent coaching that the corporation might make available, there is also an opportunity to link up by phone or e-mail with a trained and certified QEMS coach, who would NOT be a company employee, and would be, therefore, independent. This coach might be able assist the person to work through the issues being raised on the worksheet as well as others that may be connected.

## Seen As Part of A Benefits Package

QEMS should be presented to the workforce not as a conflict- resolution system, nor even as a management tool of any kind, but as the **benefit** that it truly is. The reality is that every person would be receiving a powerful tool for personal growth that, if they went outside to purchase it in the form of a workshop or program, it would cost them many hundreds, if not thousands, of dollars.

## For Use In All Areas of Life

Everyone should be encouraged to use QEMS at home as well as at work, even on issues that would seem to have nothing to do with work. These issues might include marital and relationship problems, prosperity issues, family issues and so on. (These are precisely the kinds of issues that get acted out at work and cause problems.)

## Perceiving the Benefits to the Corporation

Though QEMS will be presented as a personal benefit, employees will also come to understand, initially at the introductory seminar they will receive when the program is implemented or when they join the company, that by becoming more aware of their own issues and in taking steps to deal with them through this technology, they will be contributing greatly to the energy flow within the corporation. They will see how, by using QEMS, they will be helping to create an atmosphere of peace and harmony in the workplace. They will also see how racial tension (assuming that it is a pre-existing problem) will be reduced.

## A Top-Down Approach

Everyone in the corporation should therefore be encouraged to use this technology regularly as a way to keep the energy flowing cleanly. The program will not work if it is not thoroughly understood, fully supported and enthusiastically used by **everyone** in the company from the CEO down.

## Management Training

Supervisors, managers and executives should be given special training to be able to recognize when the Q-Work tools might need to be used and by whom. They should receive training in how to encourage people to make use of the program to defuse a situation, handle a personality clash, or take the heat out of a conflict — preferably before it even begins. One or more people in the Human Resources Department will need extended training in order to be able to run in-house seminars and trainings, as well as to provide personal coaching to those who need it.

## Mandatory as Part of a Grievance Procedure.

It might even be good policy, especially once the technology is well established and in fairly regular use and people are comfortable using it, to make Q-Work a mandatory part of any procedure that deals with grievances and conflicts. The idea would be that if a supervisor detects tension or sees a situation developing, he or she might well suggest to the people involved that they go do their Q-Work. In that sense the Q-Work might be regarded at least as a "cooling off" technique. In reality, whether the people realize it or not, the technology will be working at a much deeper level than mere cooling off and may neutralize the situation automatically.

# 12
# How it Works

The QEMS process is simple and quick — and yet the results are nothing short of dramatic. So much so, in fact, that one is left wondering how on earth such a simple technology can possibly be so potent as to be capable not only of dissolving a current conflict in the workplace when it arises but of doing such things as bringing closure to an old wound or dissolving a toxic core- negative belief that one may have been holding onto for years.

## A Homeopathic System

The best way to explain this subtle power, I think, is to refer to yet another medical analogy — homeopathy. This is another form of energy medicine that has endured, like acupuncture, for around 7,000 years. It is hard to imagine that a system of medicine would last that long if it didn't work. (Modern allopathic medicine has only been in existence for about 300 years.)

## The Homeopathic Remedy

A homeopathic remedy is made by putting into a very large amount of pure water, or alcohol mixture, a minute drop of the substance that might have upset you in the first place, the principle being that *like heals like*. Then a tiny amount of that water is taken out and put into another very large batch of pure water or alcohol mixture.

## The Energy Imprint Remains

This process is repeated over and over, the idea being to dilute the mixture to the point where, if you put it under the microscope, there would be absolutely no trace of the rogue substance present. What remains, however, is the subtle energetic imprint of the original substance. The body recognizes the energetic pattern and uses that information to balance itself naturally. This is clearly a very subtle, but extremely potent, process.

It is much the same thing with a conflict. Like any illness, a conflict is a signal that something is out of balance. The willingness to be open to the idea that the conflict is simply representative of a deeper issue trying to come to the surface to be released creates a characteristic energetic imprint or wave form of its own. Our spiritual intelligence carries that wave into the unified field which, as we already know, exists outside of the space-time continuum. As a consequence, a shift occurs and balance is automatically restored.

## Skeptics Welcome

Now just as a skeptic would say that it is impossible that a homeopathic remedy, which appears to be nothing more than water, could heal anybody of anything, so would a skeptic look at one of the QEMS tools and say that it was impossible that such simple instruments could transform someone's life.

### Not Physical Science

The answer to both of our skeptics would be more or less the same. Neither the homeopathic remedy nor the QEMS tools operate at the level of physicality. The way they work cannot be explained by the physical sciences — but we know they work. The homeopathic remedy works because it acts on what is known as the etheric body — the completely invisible energetic template for the physical body. The spiritual intelligence implicit in the etheric body registers the energetic imprint and then tells the body what to do.

The QEMS tool does the very same thing for the person in upset. The energy patterns that hold their stories, their wounds, and their memories of being hurt, abused, abandoned, betrayed, etc., are imprinted in that etheric body, and the mere act of doing the QEMS process is a subtle but potent energetic communication to the etheric body and the subconscious mind to release those patterns and to restore energy flow.

As we have said before, skeptics are more than welcome, for QEMS has no requirement that the person doing it have any belief about it or faith in it whatsoever. It's simply a matter of doing it and observing the results.

# Part Four
## The Benefits

# 13
# The Value Added

The benefits that a corporation will derive from using a system that enables it to manage subtle energy (humanergy) are many and varied. All will contribute to an increase in productivity, efficiency and profits. There is no discernible downside.

Some of the benefits will be verifiable and quantifiable, even in the short term. Others will likely have to be inferred by observing subtle changes that occur over time.

The positive changes that are likely to occur for the corporation will come about not so much from anything structural that the company does (other than simply installing the system) but from the automatic "change in vibration" that takes place within each individual as a result of their using it. Let me explain.

In Part One, we recognized that each individual has their own energy field and that each one of those contributes to the overall energy field of the corporation. In that sense, the corporation is, energetically, truly the sum of its parts. But what we know about energy fields of any kind is that they vibrate at certain frequencies. The lower the vibration, the more dense the field. Conversely, the higher the vibration, the less dense the field.

187

## Low-Vibration People

A person whose energy field vibrates at a low frequency is likely to be much more of a drag on a corporation than a person with a higher vibration. This is because the kinds of emotions that lower a person's vibration are anger, fear, resentment, jealousy, cynicism, apathy and other negative emotions. The kinds of ideas and beliefs that lower a person's vibration are precisely those kinds of core-negative beliefs given in Chapter Five that QEMS is designed to neutralize.

People with a low vibration tend to be energy vampires. They will suck energy from whatever source they can find. They have a tendency always to take more out of a system than they contribute.

[There are physical things that lower a person's vibration too — such as eating junk food, overeating, abusing drugs, not exercising and so on, but that is beyond the scope of this book].

## High-Vibration People

A person with a high vibration is likely to be free of most negative emotions and will have a predominance of core-positive beliefs. He or she is likely to be bright, happy, open-minded, likable, clear, co-operative and creative. High-vibration people are more apt to experience emotions like appreciation, gratitude, compassion, humility and love than those of a more negative nature. They are more likely to draw on the finer energy coming from Spirit and eschew energy that emanates from Ego. People of high vibration usually have high integrity.

High-vibration people tend to put a lot more into a system than they take out. They give energy to those around them rather than seek to draw it from others. It feels good to be in their presence.

Those who begin using QEMS on a regular basis will automatically raise their vibration and begin adding more value to the corporation right away. How and why this occurs will become clearer when we examine the relative vibratory rate of particular qualities of mind and associated emotions.

## A Vibratory Scale

The chart below outlines a model of how individual qualities of mind rank in terms of vibration. This information is taken from the work of David Hawkins, M.D., Ph.D., and his ground-breaking book, *Power vs. Force,* in which he has logged, in rank order, how each quality of mind scores on a scale of one to a thousand.

| Quality | Log | Emotion |
|---|---|---|
| Peace | 600 | Bliss |
| Joy | 540 | Serenity |
| Love | 500 | Reverence |
| Reason | 400 | Understanding |
| Acceptance | 350 | Forgiveness |
| Willingness | 310 | Optimism |
| Neutrality | 250 | Trust |
| Courage | 200 | Affirmation |
| Pride | 175 | Scorn |
| Anger | 150 | Hate |
| Desire | 125 | Craving |
| Fear | 100 | Anxiety |
| Grief | 75 | Regret |
| Apathy | 50 | Despair |
| Guilt | 30 | Blame |
| Shame | 20 | Humiliation |

**Fig. 14:** David Hawkins, M.D., Ph.D — Scale of Consciousness

## 200 — The Pivot Point

The critical point on the scale is the 200 mark. At less than 200, the person's main concern is personal survival and they will tend to take more out of a system than they put in. Their effect on the overall energy field of the corporation is liable therefore to be net-negative. Someone above the 200 mark is more likely to begin to consider the welfare of others as well as their own, and are likely, therefore, to have a net-positive effect on the overall energy field of the corporation.

(**Note:** This is quite independent of rank or position in the company. It is just as likely for a highly paid senior executive to be under the 200 mark as an hourly paid person in production. Neither is it a question of mental intelligence, educational level or class).

To put this in perspective, Hawkins points out that the vast majority of the world's population is well below the 200 mark. However, because the few people vibrating at very high levels (400+) are counteracting the energy of the majority vibrating below 200, the average, Hawkins claims, is 207. It has only in the last decade passed the 200 mark.

## Not Good or Bad

The idea is not to judge anyone as less than or better than someone else, good or bad. As Hawkins says:

> "Moralistic judgments are merely a function of the viewpoint from which they proceed. We see, for instance, that a person in Grief, which calibrates at a low level of 75, will be in a much better condition if he rises to Anger, which calibrates at 150. Anger, itself a destructive emotion, is still a low state of consciousness, but as social history shows, apathy can imprison entire subcultures as well as individuals. If the hopeless can

190

come to want something better (Desire — 125) and use the energy of Anger at 150 to develop Pride (175), they may then be able to take the step to Courage which calibrates at 200, and proceed to improve their individual or collective conditions."

## The Journey

We can all fall prey — temporarily, we hope — to these lower states of mind, no matter who we are. In fact such an experience can be, in itself, part of the process of raising our vibration. Our spiritual intelligence might create a crisis (our dark night of the soul) that will take us down to a very low level before bringing us up to a higher level than the one we were on prior to the crisis.

## Bob Pearson's Journey

We saw this in the Gico story where the president of the company, Bob Pearson, descended to the level of Grief and almost, but not quite, to the level of Apathy. But his own spiritual intelligence, which had been instrumental in taking him there, gave him enough of a kick start to push him back up the scale — moving quickly through **Anger** (by firing Dennis), **Pride** and **Courage** (by believing in himself and reasserting his authority), right through to **Willingness** and **Acceptance** (creating an atmosphere in the company of mutual support, forgiveness and understanding).

## The Company Goes Along Too

This is precisely what QEMS is designed to do. Negative humanergy lowers our vibration and keeps it low all the time. In Bob Pearson's case, it was his core-negative belief, created through being traumatized by his grandfather's death when Bob was only five years of age, that things would always go bad after five years. He had lived that belief out, as a pattern, all through his career. By using a tool that neutralized that belief, he freed himself to go to a vibration that was more natural for him — and to take the company up a notch or two in the process.

191

Because Bob Pearson was in a pivotal position within the company, the effect this had on the company was dramatic — literally the difference between survival and disaster. But the same thing is true all the way down the line to the lowest-paid worker. You never know how a person might add value as a result of raising their vibration.

### A Worker With High Vibration

A few years ago, I was facilitating a training along these same lines for a firm of about fifty people. They made a health-food product. Towards the end of the training, the lowest-paid worker, a quiet, unassuming young man who worked in the shipping department, spoke up for the first time that day and said the following words:

> "I have never told anyone this before because I always felt I would be laughed at and ridiculed forever if I did. But I am willing to risk doing so now, in the light of what we have done today.

> "When I am putting together someone's order, I visualize them and try to feel love for them. Then as I put the bottle in the box, I include that love energy. As I close the lid of the box, I visualize the person at the other end opening the box and being bathed in that vibration of love.

> "It's the only thing that makes this job satisfying, otherwise it would seem boring and meaningless to me. By doing this I feel I am contributing to others as well as myself."

He was clearly a person of very high vibration and, as the lowest-paid person in the company, was nevertheless adding extraordinary value to the company, its customers and himself. I suggested to the CEO that he double that man's salary and to make sure he never let him go.

Someone else with a low vibration, concerned only about getting through the day doing a boring, routine, meaningless job and feeling angry about how little he was being paid, would have added little or no value at all. His or her contribution would probably have been net-negative.

It is my contention that the QEMS program will raise the vibration of most, if not all, the people working in the company. The added value will be considerable. Even if quite a number don't use it much, it won't matter because, according to Hawkins, one person vibrating at a high level will counteract hundreds of people vibrating at under 200.

### Accountability and Responsibility
One major shift that occurs in anyone using the QEMS tools habitually is a marked increase in a sense of personal responsibility for their own life. There is no going back on this. Once we have been exposed to the concepts and ideas that are the foundation for QEMS, we really have no choice other than to stop criticizing ourselves and others, stop reacting to other people's judgments as if they were true, and stop allowing others to define who we are. We become accountable to ourselves and take responsibility for how others act towards us. In short, we give up our addiction to the victim mentality.

### Victim Mentality
In victim mentality, there is a conviction that someone else has done something bad to you, and as a direct result, they are *ipso-facto* to blame and totally responsible for the fact that you are unhappy. The principal emotion associated with victim mentality is anger.

### Perpetrator Mentality
A perpetrator mentality is the same thing as victim mentality except you now see yourself as the cause of someone else's unhappiness.

193

The principal emotion associated with the perpetrator mentality is guilt or shame.

Paradoxically, this mentality, in both its forms, is devoid of any sense of personal responsibility or accountability for what happens in one's life. There is no sense of being accountable to oneself for having created the situation jointly with the other people involved as part of the divine plan.

## Willingness is High-Vibration

When you open your mind to the possibility that everything happens for a reason and to the notion that what is done TO you is actually done FOR you, your victim mentality is transformed. Not, I hasten to add, because you have figured out WHY or even because you understand the full meaning of what you are becoming open to.

No, the transformation occurs solely because of your willingness to entertain that possibility. Notice how high up the scale of consciousness willingness is (310). Blame, the fuel of victim consciousness and the life-blood of the legal system, vibrates at a mere 30.

## Empowerment

When people become open to this new way of looking at the world and themselves in it, they simply have no choice but to begin to accept that they have a strong hand in creating their own reality, and hence, their own lives. They can't help but realize that most of what they judge and criticize is determined by their own perceptions.

Out of this realization they develop a sense of empowerment. They recognize that nothing "out there" has control over their life. Instead of seeing themselves as the "effect" in a cause-and-effect world, they realize that they are the "cause." This has the effect of raising their vibration to a level that would be impossible to achieve without the kind of shift in understanding and awareness that QEMS engenders in people purely as a result of it use.

With the installation of QEMS, so long as everyone at all levels is committed to the idea and encourages its use, a firm would expect to notice the following differences, some in the short term, others more long term, but significant nevertheless.

## • People Acting More Responsibly

More responsible behavior will be the result of what has been described in the preceding paragraphs. The changes may be imperceptible at first, but as people become more accountable to themselves and responsible for their lives, they make better decisions both for themselves and those around them. They will be seen to be adding more value.

## • Decreased Incidences of Overt Hostility and Conflict

One would expect to see a dramatic decrease in hostility and incidences of conflict at all levels — between individuals, groups, departments, customers and vendors, unions and management and so on. This is probably the easiest of all improvements to measure, assuming that there has been a procedure for recording such incidents in the past.

## • Less Blaming And Finger Pointing

When people become more self-accountable, they stop projecting and laying blame. It just doesn't serve them any more because they have given up their addiction to the victim mentality that gave rise to blaming and projecting in the first place. They become more solution oriented and forward looking.

## • More Win-Win and Fewer Zero-Sum Games

Hawkins points out that people who vibrate below 200 are at survival level and only looking out for themselves. Naturally, therefore, they will always look for ways to play the win-lose, zero-sum, game. This is where people always expect to win at someone else's expense. It's all about them and how successful they can become, no matter at what expense to others or to the greater good.

When people rise above 200, Hawkins says, their concerns tend to move towards the welfare of others as well as themselves. They will therefore be more inclined to look for win-win situations where everyone gains and no one loses. They become more oriented towards cooperation and team work and more inclined towards mutual support and caring.

## • Less Covert Sabotage of Self and Others
Sabotage is very subtle and difficult to spot unless you know what to look for. It's even more difficult to quantify. One needs to look for patterns that indicate it, but the idea is that QEMS will automatically take care of it by neutralizing the underlying cause.

## • Less Acting Out of Subconscious Issues
The longer QEMS is in use, the more likely it will be that unconscious humanergy will be neutralized. The need for it to be acted out in the workplace will therefore be eliminated.

## • Marked Increase in Morale
When people begin to take responsibility for their life, they feel empowered and feel better about themselves. According to Hawkins, when one's vibration is raised beyond the 200 mark, one begins to have concern for others and for the community in which one works. As people let go of blaming, grouching and whining, they look for ways to contribute. They simply feel better and contribute more.

## • Greater Sense of Togetherness
As we saw in Chapter One, if a person's energy field is in sync with the energy fields of those around them, there is attraction, caring and, ultimately, bonding. This can totally transform the atmosphere and hence the energy of a corporation.

## • A More Willing and Flexible Workforce

A happier, more responsible and self-accountable workforce is likely to be more flexible, adaptable and less resistant to change and growth than one that is self-absorbed, uncertain and dependent on the status quo. But at the same time, firms should be ready to capitalize on the desire of many to be more involved and willing to contribute in a new way.

## • A Marked, Short-term Increase in Attrition Rates

Some people simply don't want to give up their victim mentality, and they become uncomfortable when the people around them begin to grow and change for the better. They usually leave within about six to twelve months, but they are quickly replaced by people with a higher vibration. That's because like attracts like. These new hires will be attracted by the high vibration of the company as a whole, and they, in turn, will contribute to raising its vibration even higher. The effect is cumulative.

## • A Marked Decrease in Attrition Rates

Once the initial shake-out has occurred and the low-vibration people have been replaced by those who resonate at a higher frequency, matching that of the corporation as a whole, people will not leave. They will stay because they are happier and more fulfilled.

# 14
# Congruency

If the Quantum Energy Management System truly adds value in the ways described in the previous chapter, then, clearly, any company or institution that installs it stands to reap a great deal of benefit from it. Productivity is likely to rise as a result of having all four forms of energy (data, materials, money and humanergy), flowing more easily and more freely through the organization than before, and this situation is bound to have a positive effect on the bottom line.

## Alignment of Philosophy
However, the value that the corporation or institution will derive from using this program depends on how congruent people throughout the organization are in its use and the value they put on it. If the management style of the company is not in alignment with the underlying philosophy of the program, then less will be gained. If, on the other hand, the management style is such that it aligns with the program's philosophy, then the long-term gains could be staggering.

This means, then, that everyone, from the CEO down, must be willing to use the program so that they personally experience the results it might have on their own state of mind and on how they behave, both at home and at work. Then they will be able to relate to, and be in sync with, what is happening to everyone else in the company.

## Adjusting Policies and Procedures

Remember, a corporation is a complex set of interrelating energy fields. If any one of the fields changes, the others must change too in order to accommodate to the altered arrangement of energy within the system. This means that all parts of the organization must be sensitive to the energetic changes that begin to occur as the people change.

## More Sensitive Handling of Conflict

The first structural and procedural change that might need to occur is in how conflicts are perceived and handled within the company. Traditional conflict-resolution techniques have naturally assumed that everyone is in victim-mentality mode. That might not now always be the case.

Some sensitivity training for staff might be necessary, so that a person trying to mediate or resolve a conflict is able to recognize where a person involved is coming from energetically. Someone who has a degree of accountability and awareness of how we create conflicts as healing opportunities will need to be handled very differently from someone who is unconscious in this regard.

## Relating Differently

The overall way that the corporation relates to people will need to shift over time as more and more people become less victim-oriented, more self-accountable and more caring. The other side of that kind of personal growth is that they will have more secure boundaries, will be more free thinking, and will be far less dependent on outside authority for guidance on integrity issues, and less co-dependent.

That means employees are less likely to put up with being unfairly or badly treated or will resist doing things that are harmful and out of integrity just because they are instructed to do so. Management would be wise to be sensitive to that dynamic and take steps to ensure that they listen carefully to such people, for those people will likely be the wayshowers for how the corporation can continue to raise its vibration.

This again highlights why it is important that everyone in the company engages in the use of QEMS — so that everyone grows and changes together. Change will happen organically that way and with a lot less resistance. The corporation or institution will simply find itself moving in a new direction that will feel right. So long as everyone, particularly those in positions of authority, is in alignment, the policies and procedures will adjust accordingly. It will be evidence of **spiritual intelligence at work!**

# Appendix I

## Humanergy Dynamics at Gico — An Analysis

Assuming that you have read both the Gico Story and the accompanying material that argues the case for there being such a thing as humanergy, we thought it might be fun to briefly analyze how we think humanergy might have been operating in the Gico story and to what effect. But first, a couple of general points.

### Typical or Not

I would not be surprised if you thought that the lives of the characters in the story were not typical, in that they all seem to have had abusive and/or alcoholic parents and less than perfect childhoods. Well, of course, I needed to have characters like that in order to make the story juicy, but the sad truth is that a lot of children grow up in abusive households. Abuse associated with alcholism, as well as that which is not, is much more common than most people realize. That's because it is swept under the carpet and vehemently denied by family members. Meg's experience of trying to tell her mother about being sexually abused by her father, and getting shamed even more for daring to suggest such a thing, is quite typical. Research indicates that at least one in five adults in America today experienced physical or sexual abuse as a child, not to mention abuse of a verbal and emotional nature.

Having said that though, it is not only abused or wounded people who bring their humanergy to work with them. We all do. There isn't a human being on the planet who is without some toxic humanergy, and there will be times when we will wear it to work.

203

## Complexity

Even though we limited our story to just four or five players and only touched on a tiny part of what might have been present for all of them, the dynamics were nevertheless complex, subtle and difficult to fathom. Imagine trying to plot the dynamics where you have twenty or thirty players in close professional interaction on a daily basis, each acting out their core-negative beliefs and endeavouring to heal their primal wounds in the context of the workplace. It would be an impossibly complex web. Without some technology that uses an intelligence of a different nature than that we are accustomed to using, it would be impossible to do anything about it.

## Overall Energy Field of Gico, Inc.

To get back to the details of the story, there were obviously some problems with the corporate energy field dating back to the departure of the previous president. There were also some deep-rooted energy blocks existing between the sales and production departments that were not being addressed. On the contrary, these blocks were being actively and overtly fed by at least one of the executives, Dennis Barker, in his effort to overthrow Bob Pearson. That dynamic alone put a huge dent in the corporate energy field, representing an energy leak of major proportion. Morale in the company was low, and the staff were registering an awareness of Bob Pearson's downwardly spiralling performance as their president. Overall, the vibration of the company energy field was down and not conducive to high performance. Conflict, noncooperative behavior, high turnover, absenteeism, insubordination, apathy, cynicism and dissent were probably the order of the day. Energy was leaking everywhere from the company.

## Individual Energy Fields

Let's now turn our attention to each of the individuals in the story and look at how each one's own humanergy fed into the dynamics of the company and, indeed, how the company itself served as fertile ground for their healing opportunities to arise.

Remember, what we are looking for is evidence, albeit very subtle and almost always inconclusive, that spiritual intelligence is working in our lives, always providing opportunities for us to heal and grow. Since we don't yet have the sight to directly observe this intelligence in operation, the best we can do is look for clues that might imply that it is. The kind of clues we look for are:

a) Repeating patterns — similar events recurring
b) Numbers patterns like dates, intervals, ages, etc.
c) Oddities — things that just don't fit
d) Synchronicities — used to be called coincidences
e) Evidence of core-negative beliefs being lived out

Clues such as these give us reason to believe that there is an intelligence behind what seems to be occurring because the liklihood of such things happening by chance is extremely low.

## Timelines Reveal the Patterns

One of the best ways to see the patterns is to plot timelines from birth to the present time, plotting any significant events that occurred along the way. Since we have the most biographical information on Bob Pearson and Meg Smith, let's do one for each of them. In each case, the timelines offer interesting patterns that reveal the humanergy that each was bringing to work with them.

# Bob's Timeline

| | |
|---|---|
| 50 | --Dark night of the soul |
| 45 | --Bob joins Gico |
| 40 | -- Bob joins HEH. |
| 30 | --Rick's betrayal |
| 25 | --Bob and Rick's partnership |
| 20 | --Bob begins career |
| 5 | --Grandfather dies aged 51 |

Bob's life was shaped by two main forms of primal wounding. The first was the mental and emotional abuse by his father. The second was the "abandonment" by his grandfather who died when Bob was five, compounded by Bob's own guilt and feelings of responsibility for the death.

***Look at all the fives here!***

Bob's core-negative beliefs were (a) he would never really measure up and be good enough, no matter how hard he tried and (b) his world would always fall apart after five years. His pattern became creating three to four years of relative success with disaster setting in at year five. This kind of pattern is extremely common. Rick also abandoned and betrayed Bob abruptly after five years and probably represented the brother to whom Bob was always adversely compared by his father.

It is interesting to note that Bob came face to face with his own death, even though it was symbolic, at more or less the same age at which his grandfather had died. An oddity? This is not unusual. Had Bob continued on the path he was taking, he might well have died physically right on cue the following year.

# Meg's Timeline

| Age | Event |
|---|---|
| 35 | -- Present |
| 34 | --Divorces |
| 32 | -- CFS |
| 31 | --Marries #2 |
| 29 | --CFS |
| 28 | --Divorces |
| 27 | -- Caroline born. |
| | joins Gico |
| 26 | -- Meets Rick. |
| 25 | -- Marries |
| 24 | -- Raped |
| 16 | --Meg leaves home |
| 12 | --Meg confronts mother |
| 3 | -- Meg is abused by father |

The primal wound that shaped Meg's life was the sexual abuse at age three. Notice how the number three (or multiples thereof) feature in her life story, mostly as intervals in years between related events. Abused at 3, shamed by mother at 12, raped at 24, affair with Rick at 27. Married twice for three years and three year intervals between bouts of Chronic Fatigue Syndrome. This is a very typical pattern for an abuse victim.

She was used and abused by her father, by a rapist, and by both husbands. Even though she decided to avoid men, she "created" Monty, who did the same. Remember, he, inexplicably it seemed, turned on her after three years (an oddity). Even he couldn't understand why, but she, in effect, had recreated her father in Monty, and was acting out again the power struggle that had ensued when she reached age three. Monty, for his part, was acting out his rage with his mother.

Her chronic fatigue was probably directly related to having been raised by an obsessive-compulsive and ultra-critical mother who made her believe that whatever she did would never be enough. That is a typical belief underlying CFS. People with CFS invariably had perfectionist mothers. "No matter how hard I try, I'll never be enough."

## The Impact

Let's now look at the latent humanergy that was acted out at work by each of the players in this story and make an assessment of how it impacted the company they worked for.

## Bob — A Danger to Gico's Survival

Most of Bob's humanergy was revealed in the foregoing story, but basically he was acting out, every five years, the trauma of losing his grandfather when Bob was five and the belief that he had formed at that age, namely, that everything would fall apart after five years. The reason that his grandfather was so important to Bob is that he was his only source of love and approval.

The interesting thing here is that, but for Bob's natural intelligence and strong unconscious need to succeed in order to gain his father's approval, he would have been stuck in a downward spiral of failure. As it was, his native wit and foresight had somehow saved him on each occasion, usually by creating a sideways move just before the world crashed in on him. In that way, he had managed to keep operating at a fairly high level in the corporate world. He also, as far as we know, did not have failure with his women.

It was male energy that deserted him. There's nothing more masculine than a corporation. A corporation failed him every five years. What we don't know, of course, is what happened to HEH, Inc., when Bob bailed after having brought it to its low point. He may have ruined the company for all we know. On the other hand, having served Bob by enabling him to recreate his failure scenario, HEH, Inc. may have revived itself immediately.

Without a doubt, Bob Pearson was an extremely dangerous proposition for Gico. On paper, and in person, he appeared to be an ideal candidate to lead any small or medium-sized company. No one would ever suspect that he had a powerful unconscious need to bring any company he worked for to its knees, simply in order that he could be right about his core-negative belief. He, himself, would never have suspected it either.

But that is where he and Gico were headed, for sure, and disaster would probably have occurred had he not been exposed to the kind of technology that neutralized the core-negative belief. It is a chilling tale, but it happens all the time.

## Dennis

Clearly the more senior a person is in the company, the more effect such humanergy has. Dennis Barker's latent humanergy, based on and energized at the deepest level by his subconscious shame about his family and his roots, fueled his insatiable need to be number one. Clearly that need was toxic to the company. He created disharmony and sowed the seeds of discontent wherever and whenever he could in order to undermine Bob Pearson.

## Meg

Seniority is not the only measure of how damaging humanergy can be. Meg was junior but her humanergy was potent, albeit more subtle than Bob's. Her core-negative belief, stemming from her abuse, required that she create men who would turn on her after about three years. She had given up on romantic associations since they all had done just that, so, having failed to see the gift in the romantic associations, she (her spiritual intelligence) had "enrolled" Monty Fisk to play that role for her so she might finally heal her original wound. (She eventually did when she found QEMS.)

Not only was the relationship between Monty and Meg counterproductive in itself, but it created a lot of dissent and trouble amongst the staff. Consequently, a great deal of energy was being lost through that department. Believing that this was purely the result of Meg's unconscious need to heal her abuse and Monty's willingness to play out the role of abuser is hard, right? I know.

## Monty

As for Monty Fisk himself, his humanergy was centered around his hatred of his overbearing mother, so it was not difficult for him to be abusive to Meg, since to him, at some deep unconscious level, she represented his mother. Aged forty-six, Monty had never married because of his hatred of women in general, but he did so within six months of doing QEMS. Meg did the same!

## Gwen

Gwen Harper was a walking time bomb. So long as she was on your side, her humanergy worked for you and for the company. Her need to be the caretaker, as well as her ability to be invisible but vigilant, all worked to make her a good executive secretary. But woe betide anyone who as much as hinted that women were not as important as men or who tried to undermine those for whom she felt responsible.

## Synchronicites

Interesting synchronicities occur between Gwen, Rick, Meg and Bob. Gwen was able to connect the dots. Had it not been for those connections, and Gwen's need to take care of Bob and Meg, as well as to intuit what needed to be done, the call to Rick would not have been made. Who knows what might have happened to Bob — and Gico, Inc. then. And, of course, there was that doctor who saved Rick's life. Who *was* that man?

# Appendix II

## Instructions in the Use of the Balancing "Humanergy" Worksheet

Having read the book (and it would be unwise for you to try using the worksheet without first reading the book), you will understand that should anyone upset you or trigger negative emotion, it represents an *opportunity to balance energy.* Where before you might have been sucked into the drama and become very upset, you now know you can reach for a worksheet and balance out the energies before you get drawn in too deeply. (If you should get sucked in really deep, you run the risk of losing the awareness of there being another way of perceiving the situation. Then it will not even occur to you to do a worksheet.)

If the upset is relatively minor, then the liklihood is that one worksheet will do the trick. If, on the other hand, the upset is major or seems to be resonating something deep within you such that it produces a strong response, then keep doing worksheets until the energy around the situation, person or incident dissipates.

I have structured these instructions by giving you the underlying rationale of each of the steps so that you can get a feel for why you are doing it and what the intention is. I also attempt, where I feel it is necessary, to provide some guidance in how to complete each step.

You will find an actual full-size worksheet in the back of the book. Use this to make photocopies for your own use. You will also find a CD containing the 13 Steps process. It is self-explanatory.

In the following text, the relevant parts of the worksheet are filled in as if Meg had completed it at the time she was going through one of the situations she used to find herself in with Monty Fisk, her boss at Gico. I have picked up on how Monty would always try to block her promotion and am assuming that it has happened again. This has prompted Meg to do another worksheet on Monty.

Do remember, that the worksheet is done for oneself only. It should NEVER be shared with anyone, especially the person you are doing it on. It is always best to destroy the completed worksheet for this reason. If you do keep it, make sure it is somewhere safe. For example, it would have been unwise for Meg to keep it at work.

Also, it works much better from an energetic standpoint if you say everything out loud. It frees the energy that's tied up in the throat center, held there as a consequence of not being able to express your true feelings. Meg would dearly have loved to say some choice things to Monty but could never do so because of her subordinate position. This is her chance to do so in writing — but to herself only.

## Special Acknowledgments

This worksheet has its origins in one created some years ago by Dr. Michael Ryce, a pioneer in this field who has dedicated his life to bringing the message of forgiveness to everyone on the planet, and in the work of Arnold M. Patent. Arnold originally introduced me to spiritual principle, and his work inspires many of the steps in this forgiveness worksheet. I am deeply grateful for the contributions each has made to my understanding and, by extension, to this book.

# Balancing "Humanergy" Worksheet

### A QEMS "Q-Work" tool For Transforming Potentially
### Harmful Subtle Energy

Date: **8/7/04**

**Subject (X)** The Person, or Group of People I am Upset With __

### MONTY FISK

• Identify the person, situation, or object about which you feel upset, here noted as "X." In certain circumstances it may be yourself, but there is a big trap in doing this, especially when you first start doing this work. The trap is that because guilt is at the root of all separation, we are much too inclined to beat ourselves up at every opportunity. In my workshops, I tell people not to do it for that reason. All forgiveness is self-forgiveness in the end, but it is best achieved in my opinion by forgiving and extending love outwards to others. It is universal law that it is always returned, and you discover yourself as having been forgiven.

Be sure to tell your story as if you were telling someone else what happened or is happening. Use names.

---

**1.** I am upset because ....

*Monty keeps attacking me for doing my job. Everything I do is wrong in his eyes. He is always dominating me and criticizing me. He blocked my promotion again and I am mad about that. He's always doing it. He's a controlling, mean son-of-bitch and I can hardly stand to be around him any more.*

---

**1.** Just tell the story about your upset and define the situation as you see it. Don't hold back. Describe how it feels for you right now.

Do not edit or overlay it with any spiritual or psychological interpretation. You must honor where you are now, even if you know that you are in the World of Ego, and illusion.

Even if we have raised our vibration considerably we can easily be knocked off balance and find ourselves back in the World of Ego, seeing ourselves as victims and all that goes with that. Being human requires that experience. We cannot always be joyful and peaceful and see the perfection in absolutely every situation.

> **2 (a) CONFRONTING X:** I am upset with you because:
>
> *You have blocked my promotion again, you bastard! I hate you. You are so mean and horrible to me and I don't know why.*

**2a.** Be as confrontational as possible with X, and lay out exactly what you blame him/her/it for. This section's small space only allows a few words, but let the words you choose represent the totality of your upset. If the object or situation has no name, give it one, or at least write about it as if it were a person. If the person is dead, speak to him or her as if he or she were there in front of you. If you want to write it out in full, use some additional paper This step allows you to address the person directly. However, keep to one issue. Do not discuss other things on this worksheet. Reaching your objective — balanced energy — requires you to get clarity on precisely what you feel so upset about *now*.

> **2 (b)** Because of what you *Monty* did (are doing), I feel: *(Identfy your real emotions here)*
>
> *Deeply hurt, angry, betrayed, trapped and abused. I feel very resentfull and vengefull*

**2b.** It is vitally important that you allow yourself to feel your feelings. Do not censor them or *stuff* them. Remember, we came into the physical realm to experience emotion — the essence of being human. All emotions are good, except when we suppress them. Stuffing emotion creates potentially harmful energy blocks in our bodies.

Make sure the emotions you identify represent real emotions that you actually feel, not just *thoughts* about how you feel. Are you *mad, glad, sad,* or *afraid?* If you cannot be specific, that is okay. Some people find themselves unable to differentiate one feeling from another. If that holds true for you, just notice what general emotional quality you can feel around the situation.

If you would like to feel your emotions more clearly or strongly, pick up a tennis racquet or a bat and beat the heck out of some cushions or pillows. Use something that will make a noise when you hit the cushions. If anger scares you, have someone with you when you do this exercise. That person should encourage and support you in feeling your anger (or any other emotion) and make it safe to do so. Screaming into a cushion also helps release feelings. As I have stressed many times, the more you allow yourself to feel the hurt, sadness, or fear that might lie beneath your anger, the better.

**3.** I recognize and accept my feelings without judgment. My feelings are my authentic reaction to the situation. They show me how I am perceiving it.

(Check the appropriate box),

| Willing | Open | Skeptical | Unwilling |
|---------|------|-----------|-----------|
| **X** | | | |

**3.** This important step provides you with an opportunity to allow yourself some freedom from the belief that feelings like anger, vengefulness, jealousy, envy, even sadness are bad and should be denied. No matter what they are, you need to feel your emotions in exactly the way they occur for you, for they are an expression of your true self. Your soul wants you to feel them fully. Know they are perfect, and quit judging yourself for having them.

Try the following three-step process for integrating and accepting your feelings:

1. Feel the feeling fully, and then identify it as either mad, glad, sad, or afraid.

2. Embrace the feelings in your heart just the way they are. *Accept them.* Love them as part of yourself. Let them be perfect. You cannot move into the joy vibration without first accepting your feelings and making peace with them. Say this affirmation: *"I ask for support in feeling appreciation for each of my emotions just the way they are, as I embrace it within my heart and accept it as part of myself."*

3. Now *feel appreciation for yourself* for having these feelings and know you have chosen to feel them as a way of moving your energy towards healing.

**4.** I own my feelings. No one can make me feel anything. It's my choice.

| Willing | Open | Skeptical | Unwilling |
|---------|------|-----------|-----------|
|         | X    |           |           |

**4.** This statement reminds us that no one can make us feel anything. Our emotions are our own. As we feel, recognize, accept, and love them unconditionally as part of ourselves, we become entirely free to hold on to them or let them go. This realization empowers us by helping us realize that the problem resides not *out there* but *in here*, within ourselves. This realization also represents our first step away from the victim archetype vibration. When we think other people, or even situations, make us mad, glad, sad, or afraid, we give them all our power.

**5.** Even though I don't know why or how, I now see that my spiritual intelligence has created this situation in order that I learn and grow.

| Willing | Open | Skeptical | Unwilling |
|---------|------|-----------|-----------|
|         |      | X         |           |

**5.** This is probably the most important statement on the worksheet. It reinforces the notion that thoughts, feelings and beliefs create our experiences and that furthermore, our spiritual intelligence orders our reality in such a way as to support our spiritual growth. When we open ourselves to this truth, the problem almost always disappears.

The statement challenges us to accept the possibility that the situation may be purposeful and to let go of the need to know the how and the why of it.

This is where most intellectually inclined people have the greatest difficulty. They want 'proof' before they believe anything. Therefore they make knowing 'why' a condition for accepting the situation as a healing opportunity.

This is a dead-end trap since to ask how and why things happen as they do is to ask to know the mind of God. At the level we are now in our spiritual development, we cannot possibly know the mind of God. We must give up our need to know why (which is a victim's question anyway), and surrender to the idea that God does not make mistakes and therefore everything is in Divine order.

The importance of this step comes in its ability to help you feel your way out of the victim mode into the possibility that the person, object, or situation with whom you have the issue reflects precisely that part of yourself that you have rejected and which cries out to be accepted. It acknowledges that the Divine essence within, the knowing part of yourself, your spiritual intelligence has set the situation up for you, so you can learn, grow and heal a misperception or a false belief.

This step also creates self-empowerment. Once we realize we have created a situation, we have the power to change it. We can choose to see ourselves as the victim of circumstance, or we can choose to see our circumstance as an opportunity to learn and to grow and to have our lives be the way we want.

*Do not judge yourself for creating a situation.* Remember, the Divine part of yourself created it. If you judge the Divine part of you, you judge God. Acknowledge yourself as a wonderful, creative, Divine being with the ability to create your own lessons along the spiritual path, lessons that eventually will take you home. Once you are able to do this, you are able to surrender to the Divine essence that you are and to trust it to do the rest.

**6.** I am noticing that this situation shows similarities to other situations that happened in the past, which clues me in to the fact that this might be a healing opportunity. *For example, it reminds me of......*

*Every man I have ever had or been around has abused me in some way, always overpowering me, including my father and two husbands. They all betrayed me after three years. All men are untrustworthy and hurt me.*

**6.** This step recognizes that we are curious human beings and that we have an insatiable need to know why things happen as they do. So having said above that we must abandon our need to know, this step offers us the chance to have some fun looking for some of the more obvious clues that would offer us evidence that the situation always was perfect in some unexplainable way. So long as we do not make having such evidence a prerequisite for accepting that this was so, there is no harm in it, and it may turn on some light bulbs. Bear in mind, too, that there may well be nothing that strikes you as evidence one way or the other. If nothing stands out, don't worry. Just leave the box blank and go on to the next item on the worksheet. It does NOT mean that the statement is any less true.

The kind of clues to look out for might be as follows:

**1. Repeating Patterns:** This is the most obvious one. Marrying the same kind of person over and over again is an example. Picking life partners who are just like your mother or father is another. Having the same kind of event happening over and over is a clear signal. People doing the same kind of things to you, like letting you down or never listening to you, is another clue that you have an issue to heal in that area.

**2. Number Patterns:** Not only do we do things repetitively, but often do so in ways that have a numerical significance. We may lose our job every two years, fail in relationships every nine years, always create relationships in threes, get sick at the same age as our parents, find the same number turning up in everything we do, and so on. It is very helpful to construct a time-line like the one I did for Jill — page 36 of the Radical Forgivness book, except that you might fill in all the dates and note all intervals of time between certain events. You might well find a meaningful timewise correlation in what is happening.

**3. Body Clues:** Your body is giving you clues all the time. Are you always having problems on one side of your body or in areas that correlate to particular chakras and the issues contained therein, for example? Books by Caroline Myss, Louise Hay and many others will help you find meaning in what is happening to your body and what the healing message is. In our work with cancer patients, for example, the cancer always turned out to be a loving invitation to change or to be willing to feel and heal repressed emotional pain.

**4. Coincidences and 'Oddities.'** This is a rich field for clues. Anytime anything strikes you as odd or out of character, not quite as you'd expect or way beyond chance probability, you know you are onto something. For example, not only was it odd that, in Jill's story, both girls who were getting the love that Jill felt was denied her were called Lorraine, which is not a common name in England, they were also both blonde, blue-eyed, and the first born of three. Jeff's behavior was also extremely uncharacteristic. Far from being cruel and insensitive, Jeff is an exceedingly kind, nurturing, and sensitive man. I can't imagine Jeff being cruel to anyone. His behavior towards Jill certainly struck me as odd in the extreme.

Where once we thought things happened by chance and were just coincidences, we are now willing to think that it is Spirit making things happen synchronistically for our highest good. It is these synchronicities that lie embedded in our stories, and once we see them as such, we become free then to feel the truth in the statement that "my spiritual intelligence has created this situation in order that I learn and grow."

---

**7.** My discomfort is my signal that I am withholding love from myself and (X) *Monty* by judging, holding expectations, wanting (X) *Monty* to change and seeing (X) *Monty* as less than perfect. I now realize that I will find peace only when I let go of these unreasonable demands and accept him/her/them just the way they are. *(List the judgments, expectations and behaviors that indicate you were wanting (X) to change).*

*I am judging him to be a mean person and abusive to me. My pain is in wanting him to treat me differently. I am wanting him to treat me now like he did during my first three years at the firm.*

---

**7.** When we feel disconnected from someone, we cannot love them. When we judge a person (or ourselves) and make them wrong, we withhold love. Even when we make them right, we are withholding love, because we make our love conditional upon their *rightness* continuing.

Any attempt to change someone involves a withdrawal of love, because wanting them to change implies that they are wrong (need to change) in some way. Furthermore, we may even do harm in encouraging them to change, for though we may act with the best

221

intentions, we may interfere with their spiritual lesson, mission, and advancement.

This is more subtle than we realize. For instance, if we send unsolicited healing energy to someone because they are sick, we are in effect making a judgment that they are not OK as they are and should not be sick. Who are we to make that decision? Being sick may be the very experience they need to have for their spiritual growth. Naturally if they request a healing, then it becomes a different matter entirely, and you do all you can in response to their request. Nevertheless, you still see them as perfect.

So make a note in this box of all the ways in which you want the person you are forgiving to be different or in what respects you want them to change. What subtle judgments do you make about the person which indicate your inability to accept them just the way they are? What behavior do you exhibit that shows you to be in judgment of them? You may be quite surprised to find that your well-intentioned desire for them to be different 'for their own benefit,' was really just a judgment on your part.

If the truth be known, it is precisely your judgment that creates his or her resistance to changing. Once you let go of the judgment, her or she will probably change. Ironic isn't it?

**8.** I now realize that I get upset only when someone resonates in me those parts of myself I have disowned, denied, repressed and projected onto them. X *Monty* is reflecting what I need to love and accept in myself. Thanks X. *Monty*

| Willing | Open | Skeptical | Unwilling |
|---------|------|-----------|-----------|
| X | | | |

**8.** These statements acknowledge that when we get upset with someone, they are invariably reflecting back to us the very parts of ourselves that we most despise and have projected onto them.

If we can open ourselves enough to be willing to accept that this person is offering us a chance to accept and love a part of ourselves that we have condemned and that he or she is a healing angel in that sense, the work will have been done.

And as we have said before, you don't have to like the person. Just recognize them as a mirror, thank their soul by doing this worksheet, and move on.

Neither do we need to figure out what parts of ourselves are being mirrored. Usually it is far too complicated anyway. Let it go at that, and don't be drawn into an analysis. It works best without it.

**9.** In forgiving (X), *Monty* I find love for myself.

| Willing | Open | Skeptical | Unwilling |
|---------|------|-----------|-----------|
| X | | | |

**9.** This statement reminds us that through our stories which are always full of misperceptions, we create our reality and our lives. We will always draw people to us who will mirror our misperceptions and offer us the opportunity to heal the error and move in the direction of truth.

**10.** I now realize that nothing (X), or anyone else, has done is either right or wrong. I drop all judgment.

| Willing | Open | Skeptical | Unwilling |
|---------|------|-----------|-----------|
|         |      | X         |           |

**10.** This step goes against everything that we have ever been taught about being able to distinguish between right and wrong, good and evil. After all, the whole world gets divided up along those lines. Yes, we know that the World of Humanity is really just an illusion, but that doesn't alter the fact that human experiences demand that we make these particular distinctions in our daily lives.

What helps us with this step is realizing that we are only affirming that there is no right or wrong, good or bad when seeing things from the spiritual big-picture standpoint — from the perspective of the World of Spirit. From there we are able to get beyond the evidence of our senses and minds and see Divine purpose and meaning in everything. Once we are able to see that, then we can see that there is no right or wrong. It just is.

**11.** I release the need to blame and to be right, and I am WILLING to see the spiritual intelligence in the situation.

| Willing | Open | Skeptical | Unwilling |
|---------|------|-----------|-----------|
| X       |      |           |           |

**11.** This step confronts you with the spiritual intelligence in the situation and tests your willingness to see the perfection in it. While it never will be easy to see the good in something such as child abuse, we can nevertheless be *willing* to imagine that there might be some kind of perfection in the situation, be *willing* to drop the judgment, and be *willing to drop the need to be right.* While it may always be difficult to recognize that both the abuser and the abused somehow created their situation to learn a lesson at the soul level, and that their mission was to transform the situation on behalf of all abused people, we can nevertheless be *willing* to entertain this thought.

Obviously, the closer we are to a situation, the more difficult it becomes to see its perfection, but seeing the perfection does not always mean understanding it. We cannot know the reasons why things happen as they do; we must simply have faith that they are happening perfectly and for the highest good of all.

Observe your strong need to be right. We possess an enormous investment in being right, and we learned at an early age to fight to be right, which usually means proving that someone else is wrong. We even measure our self worth by how often we are right; thus it is no wonder that we have such trouble accepting that something just *is* — that it is neither inherently right nor wrong. If you really cannot at this point drop your judgment about something that seems awful, just reconnect with your feelings (see step #3 above), move into them, and admit to yourself that you cannot yet take this step. However, *be willing* to drop your judgment. Willingness always remains the key. Willingness creates the energetic imprint of Radical Forgiveness. As the energy shifts, all else follows.

**12.** Even though I may not understand what it was, I now realize that you and I have both been receiving exactly what we each had subconsciously chosen and were doing a healing dance with and for each other, orchestrated by our spiritual intelligence.

| Willing | Open | Skeptical | Unwilling |
|---------|------|-----------|-----------|
|         | X    |           |           |

**12.** This statement serves as yet another reminder of how we can instantly become aware of our subconscious beliefs if we look at what shows up in our lives. What we have at any particular point in time truly *is what we want.* We have, at the soul level, chosen our situations and experiences, and our choices are not wrong. And this is true for all parties involved in the drama. Remember, there are no villains or victims, just players. Each person in the situation is getting exactly what he or she wants.

225

**13.** I bless you (X) *Monty* for being willing to play a part in my growth and honor myself for being willing to play a part in yours. I feel now that, in some mysterious way, we have both gained from this experience.

| Willing | Open | Skeptical | Unwilling |
|---------|------|-----------|-----------|
| **X** |  |  |  |

**13.** It is entirely appropriate to bless (X) for co-creating the situation with you so you could become aware of the beliefs that create your life. (X) deserves your gratitude and blessings since this co-creation and subsequent awareness gives you the ability to know your beliefs, which in turn, empowers you with the ability to let them go. When you do so, you can make another choice immediately about your beliefs and what you want to create in your life. (X) is entitled to feel the same gratitude for the same reasons.

**14.** I release from my consciousness all feelings of: (as in box 2b)

*hurt, anger, betrayal, being trapped and abused., resentfull and vengefull*

**14.** This enables you to affirm that you release the feelings that you had noted in Box 2. As long as these emotions and thoughts remain in your consciousness, they block your awareness of the misperception that is causing the upset. If you still feel strongly about the situation, you still have an investment in whatever the misperception is — your belief, interpretation, judgment, etc. Do not judge this fact or try to change your investment. Just notice it.

Your emotions about your situation may come back time and time again, and you can make that okay, too. Just be willing to feel them and then release them, at least for the moment, so the light of awareness can shine through you and allow you to see the misperception. Then, once again, you can choose to see the situation differently.

226

Releasing emotions and corresponding thoughts serves an important role in the forgiveness process. As long as those thoughts remain operative, they continue lending energy to our old belief systems, which created the reality we now are trying to transform. Affirming that we release both the feeling and the thoughts attached to them begins the healing process.

---

**15.** I now realize that what I was experiencing (my victim story and the pain associated with it) was the result of how I was framing (interpreting) the situation. I now understand that I can change this 'reality' by simply reframing it in spiritual terms and being willing to see the perfection in the situation. For example........ *(Attempt a Radical Forgiveness reframe which may simply be a general statement indicating that you just know everything is perfect or specific to your situation if you can actually see what the gift is. Note: Often you cannot and that's OK)*

*I now see that Monty was acting out for me my core - ve belief that all men will betray me and abuse me, more than likely after three years, just like my father did, and was giving me another opportunity to radically forgive my father and to fully come to the realization that in truth, and in terms of the spiritual big picture, nothing wrong happened. I am now free of the pain I created around that story and free of the need to have anyone else treat me abusively. God bless you Monty - my healing angel. I am free now.*

---

**15.** If you are not able to see a new interpretation which is specific to your situation, that's not a problem. The Radical Forgiveness reframe might simply be expressed in a very general way, such as, *"what happened was simply the unfoldment of a Divine plan. It was called forth by my own Higher Self for my spiritual growth and the people involved were doing a healing dance with me, so, in truth, nothing wrong ever happened."* Writing something like that would be perfectly adequate. On the other hand, if you did have some insights into how it all worked out in a perfect sense, that would be fine too.

What would NOT be helpful would be to write an interpretation based on assumptions rooted in the World of Humanity, like giving reasons why it happened or making excuses. You might be exchanging one BS story for another or even shifting into pseudoforgiveness.

A new interpretation of your situation should allow you to feel its perfection from the spiritual standpoint and become open to the gift it offers you. Your reframe should offer a way of looking at your situation that reveals the hand of God or Divine Intelligence working for you and showing you how much It loves you.

*Note: It may take completing many worksheets on the same issue to feel the perfection. And remember, it is a fake-it-til-you-make-it process. So if you don't feel any different towards this person after doing the worksheet, don't be concerned. It works at a very subtle energetic level — and in Spirit's time.*

*There are no right answers, no goals, no grades, and no end products here. The value lies in the process, in doing the work. Let whatever comes be perfect, and resist the urge to edit and evaluate what you write. You cannot do it wrong.*

**16.** I completely accept myself _____ *Meg* _____ as a loving, authentic, generous and creative being. I release all need to hold onto emotions and ideas of lack and limitation connected to the past.

I withdraw my energy from the past and release all grievances. I let go of all barriers against the love and abundance that I know I have in this moment.

I create my life and I am empowered to be myself again, to unconditionally love and support myself, just the way I am, in all my power and magnificence.

**16.** The importance of this affirmation cannot be overemphasized. Say it out loud, and let yourself feel it. Let the words resonate within you. Self-judgment is at the root of all our problems, and even when we have removed judgment from others and forgiven them, we continue to judge ourselves. We even judge ourselves for judging ourselves!

The difficulty we experience in trying to break this cycle results from the fact that the Ego's survival depends on our feeling guilty about who we are. The more successfully we forgive others, the more the Ego tries to compensate by making us feel guilty about ourselves. This explains why we can expect to encounter enormous resistance to moving through the forgiveness process. The Ego feels threatened at every step, and it *will* put up a fight. We see the results of this internal struggle when we do not complete a Forgiveness Worksheet, when we create more reasons to continue projecting onto X and feeling victimized, when we do not find time to meditate, or when we forget to do other things that support us in remembering who we are. The closer we get to letting go of something that elicits the feeling of guilt the more the Ego kicks and screams, thus the more difficult the forgiveness process seems.

So, be willing to go through the resistance, knowing that on the other side lies peace and joy. Be willing also to feel any pain, depression, chaos, and confusion that might occur while you are going through it.

> **17.** I now SURRENDER to the Higher Power I think of as ___*God*___ and trust in the knowledge that this situation will continue to unfold perfectly and in accordance with Divine guidance and spiritual law.
>
> I acknowledge my own spiritual intelligence and feel myself totally reconnected with my Power. I am restored to my true nature, which is LOVE, and I now restore love to (X) *Monty* ___
>
> I give thanks for this opportunity to both give and receive LOVE.

**17.** This represents the final step in the forgiveness process. However, it is *not* your step to take. You affirm that you are willing to experience it and turn the remainder of the process over to the Higher Power. Ask that the healing be completed by Divine grace and that you and X be restored to your true nature, which is love, and reconnected to your Source which is also Love.

This final step offers you the opportunity to drop the words, the thoughts and the concepts and to actually *feel* the love. When you reach the bottom line, only love exists. If you can truly tap into that love, you are home free. You need do nothing else.

So, take a few minutes to meditate on this statement and be open to feeling the love. You may have to try this exercise many times before you feel it, but one day, just when you least expect it, the love and the joy will envelop you.

**18.** As a result of doing this worksheet, I would best describe my feeling in this moment as being ...

*calm and peaceful. A sense of gratitude.*

**18.** The chances are that no matter what the feelings were at the beginning, even if they were subconscious, have changed. Check in and note in this box what it is you are feeling, if anything. But tell yourself the truth. If the feelings seem not to have changed, don't imagine that you have failed to do it right. It will still work. If you still feel angry, that's OK. If you still feel angry in another 24 hours, do another worksheet. And if you are feeling numb, don't be concerned. That is not unusual.

**19.** A Note To You (X) ___*Monty*___ "Having done this worksheet today, I....

*I realize how lucky I am to have you in my life.*
*I knew we were meant to be together for a reason*
*and now I know what it was. I release you from the*
*need to treat me like my father did.*

I completely forgive you (X) for I now realize that you did nothing wrong and that everything is in Divine order. I acknowledge, accept and love you unconditionally just the way you are.

**19.** You began the Forgiveness Worksheet by confronting (X). Your energy probably has shifted since you began, even if the shift occurred only a moment or two ago. What would you like to say to (X)? Allow yourself to write without conscious thought, if possible, and do not judge your words. Let them surprise even you.

**20.** A Note To Myself

> *I honor myself for having the courage to go through this and for being able to get beyond being the victim - I am FREE!*
>
> I recognize that I am a spiritual being having a human experience, and I love and support myself in every aspect of my humanness.

**20.** Remember, all forgiveness starts as a lie. You begin the process without forgiveness in your heart, and *you fake it until you make it.* So, honor yourself for doing it and yet be gentle with yourself, and let the forgiveness process take as long as you need. Be patient with yourself. Acknowledge yourself for the courage it takes simply to attempt completing the Forgiveness Worksheet, for you truly face your demons in the process. Doing this work takes enormous courage, willingness, and faith.